MW01644552

Foundational eDiscovery: A Practical Guide to Early Case Management

John Price

Brandon D'Agostino

First Edition
ISBN: 9798308352648
Published by: Five Rivers Media, LLC
United States
Editor: Wendy Raymond Hacker
Content Review: Doug Austin, Alisa McLellan, Allyson Haynes Stuart
Cover design: Dylan Ingram and Scott Williams

For permissions, inquiries, or additional information, please contact:
inquiries@fiveriversmedia.com

Foreword

One of the famous quotes from Sun Tzu's ***The Art of War*** is, "Every battle is won before it is fought," and it emphasizes the importance of thorough preparation and strategic planning before you go into battle. When I saw that the title of this book started with the words "Foundational eDiscovery," it was "preaching to the choir" for me. For over two decades, I've witnessed organizations struggle with eDiscovery challenges that could have been significantly mitigated by proactive planning and collaboration. Too often, eDiscovery is treated as a reactive process triggered by litigation or regulatory inquiries rather than a strategic effort built on sound information governance (IG) practices. Due to that reactive mindset, the "battle" to conduct efficient, effective eDiscovery is often lost before the case begins.

What John Price and Brandon D'Agostino have achieved in ***Foundational eDiscovery: A Practical Guide to Early Case Management*** is more than just a roadmap for winning the "battle" of effective eDiscovery; It's a blueprint for transforming IG and eDiscovery from potential liabilities into organizational strengths.

Let's face it: the digital age has brought us tremendous opportunities, but it has also introduced just as many complex challenges – none more involved than managing the ever-expanding volumes of electronically stored information (ESI). In today's fast-paced business and regulatory environment, where data flows freely across borders, platforms, and devices, organizations face a growing need to establish robust, defensible processes for eDiscovery – **before** the case begins. John and Brandon's book hits home in addressing that need.

Bridging the silos between legal, IT, and business teams isn't just a best practice – it's a necessity in today's hybrid and highly regulated work environments. Fostering collaboration is essential today to better navigate the complexities of compliance, reduce litigation risks, and leverage data as a strategic asset. This book provides not only the principles for achieving this integration but also the practical steps and actionable tips to make it a reality.

What sets this book apart is its focus on foundational concepts that remain relevant regardless of changing technologies or legal trends. From the critical importance of metadata to the intricacies of defensible deletion and data mapping, the strategies outlined here are grounded in real-world challenges and solutions. These insights will resonate with professionals across all levels of expertise—whether you're an IT specialist new to eDiscovery, a seasoned litigator seeking to optimize workflows, or a compliance officer aiming to strengthen organizational readiness.

Throughout the book also runs a theme of empowerment. Legal, IT, and business teams are empowered and encouraged to take control of their data, establish defensible practices, and respond confidently to the demands of litigation and regulatory scrutiny. But it also empowers organizations to look beyond compliance and leverage these practices for operational efficiency, cost reduction, and strategic decision-making.

The best practices promoted by John and Brandon in this book are consistent with the evolution of the eDiscovery industry toward IG being the foundation of effective discovery. The Electronic Discovery Reference Model (EDRM) model is a terrific example of that. When it was created in 2005, there was no consideration for information governance. Over the years, the model evolved to account for IG – first to an "Information Management" box, then to an "Information Management" circle, to the current model, which includes the Information Governance Reference Model (IGRM) as the perpetual "phase" that leads to eDiscovery. The IGRM itself promotes collaboration between legal, IT, and business teams, among other stakeholder groups. The best practices promoted by John and Brandon in this book are based on foundational – there's that word again! – principles that the industry has already promoted.

As your organization embarks on its journey toward better eDiscovery practices, I encourage you to embrace the lessons and strategies shared by the authors. Implement them thoughtfully, adapt them to your unique organizational context, and watch them transform how you manage information. This is not just a guide – it's a call to action for building a future where data is no longer a burden but an asset.

In the ever-evolving landscape of digital information, having a strong foundation isn't just an advantage in winning the "battle" of eDiscovery—it's a necessity. This book provides the tools to lay that foundation and build a stronger, more resilient organization.

Doug Austin, Editor of eDiscovery Today

Introduction – About This Book

Purpose of the Book

We (the authors) have worked together for a long time. There are a few recurring themes in our frequent conversations related to eDiscovery within organizations:

- Information governance impacts the eDiscovery process more than most people realize.
- There are weaknesses in the identification process that add complexity and confusion to the eDiscovery process.
- A stronger connection between business, legal, and IT will make the eDiscovery process more efficient.

This guide is designed to serve as a cornerstone for professionals navigating the complex domains of eDiscovery and information governance (IG). It aims to provide a detailed yet practical framework to help legal, IT, and compliance teams manage electronically stored information (ESI) efficiently and defensibly in litigation, regulatory inquiries, and other legal matters.

This book connects foundational principles, practical methodologies, and actionable strategies to simplify the intricate processes within the Electronic Discovery Reference Model (EDRM)[1], ensuring compliance, cost-efficiency, and operational readiness.

---

[1] *See* www.edrm.net. At the time of publication, a cross-functional committee made up of eDiscovery experts from corporations, law firms, service providers, and software companies are collaborating to develop the EDRM 2.0. References in this book to stages of the EDRM are based on the current version of the model.

What to Expect

A Structured Approach

The guide is divided into well-organized sections corresponding to the key phases of the eDiscovery lifecycle—information governance, identification, preservation, and collection. Each section begins with foundational insights and progresses into detailed methodologies and quick wins that readers can implement immediately.

As this is aimed at being an operational and practical guide, you will not see references to eDiscovery case law. This is intentional both due to the rapidly evolving nature of this body of law and the changes in technology that will no doubt prompt ongoing changes in case law for the foreseeable future. We will refer to well-settled principles of law and tailor processes defensible in most courts. However, always double-check the prevailing precedent in your jurisdiction before making any assumptions. EDiscoveryAssistant.com is a great resource for keeping up with eDiscovery decisions across the country.

Key Highlights

- **Foundational Understanding:** Introduction to essential concepts of IG and eDiscovery to provide a baseline for readers of varying expertise levels.
- **Practical Strategies:** Step-by-step guidance and tools to address legal and IT teams' real-world challenges.
- **Quick Wins:** Actionable tips to immediately improve data management and legal workflows.

- **Cross-functional Collaboration:** Emphasis on integrating efforts across legal, IT, and business units to streamline operations.

Thematic Coverage

- **Part 1: Information Governance (IG)**
  Explore IG's pivotal role in setting a proactive eDiscovery foundation. Topics include aligning legal and business needs, data mapping, defensible deletion, and implementing IG strategies for compliance and efficiency.

- **Part 2: Identification**
  Understand techniques for pinpointing relevant ESI and custodians. Learn how custodian mapping, data source identification, and early case assessments streamline eDiscovery efforts.

- **Part 3: Preservation**
  Understand the legal and technical nuances of preserving ESI. Topics include legal hold implementation, addressing spoliation risks, and the technical integrity of preserved data.

- **Part 4: Collection**
  Focus on strategies for efficient data collection, emphasizing defensibility and accuracy and leveraging advanced tools and methodologies to manage diverse data sources effectively.

- **Part 5: Preparing for Downstream Review**

  Prepare data to move from foundational eDiscovery to the remaining phases of the EDRM (processing, review, production, and presentation).

Audience

This book is tailored for business leaders, legal teams, IT professionals, compliance officers, and anyone responsible for managing ESI within or on behalf of organizations. Whether you're new to the field or looking to refine your practices, this guide offers insights to help you stay compliant, minimize risks, and improve efficiency.

Why This Guide Matters

The intersection of legal and data management is increasingly fraught with challenges due to the explosion of data, evolving regulatory requirements, and the critical need for cost-efficient, defensible workflows. This book equips readers with the tools and knowledge to navigate these challenges successfully.

By focusing on both the strategic and tactical aspects of eDiscovery and IG, this guide helps organizations transform their data from a liability into an asset, ensuring they are prepared to respond to legal inquiries and leverage their information for operational excellence.

About the Authors

John Price

John Price is a seasoned eDiscovery professional and author with over two decades of experience bridging the worlds of business, legal, and information technology. John has devoted his career to helping organizations manage data with precision, compliance, and efficiency.

Throughout his career, John has emphasized the intersection of legal frameworks, technological advancements, and practical workflows to enhance organizational capabilities in managing data. His expertise spans Information Governance (IG), eDiscovery readiness, custodian and data mapping, and data collection, reflecting a deep understanding of enterprises' challenges in today's regulatory environments.

In this book, John combines his deep understanding of IG principles and eDiscovery processes to provide a comprehensive guide for legal and IT teams. Focusing on bridging cross-functional gaps, John offers tools, techniques, and strategies that ensure defensible outcomes while meeting business and legal objectives.

Brandon D'Agostino

Brandon D'Agostino is an attorney and member of the South Carolina Bar Association. He graduated *magna cum laude* from the Charleston School of Law where he served as an editor on the *Charleston Law Review* and as a member of the school's first-ever Mock Trial Team. He also co-taught one of the first eDiscovery courses in the country as an adjunct professor at the Charleston

School of Law with Allyson Haynes Stuart. The course was developed and is still taught as a skills-based course to provide students with a working knowledge of the technical and procedural elements of eDiscovery in practice combined with a survey of eDiscovery case law. Brandon enjoys teaching and preparing the next generation of lawyers with the skills needed to navigate a developing body of law.

Brandon began his career in eDiscovery as an in-house discovery attorney in 2008. He moved into the software industry in 2009, and this was the beginning of a 15-year journey in eDiscovery, information governance, and regulatory compliance that spanned seven companies and thousands of clients. Before that, Brandon had a 10-year career in information technology which has given him a unique perspective that blends practical enterprise IT experience, legal, and business acumen.

In writing this book, Brandon hopes to provide practical guidance to the many faces of eDiscovery from legal and non-legal backgrounds who find themselves, either voluntarily or involuntarily, thrust into the heart of the beautiful chaos that is eDiscovery.

Acknowledgments

John Price

I couldn't have completed this project without an incredible support network of family, friends, and professional colleagues. This marks my first book in nearly 20 years, a significant departure from my earlier writing and a reflection of how times—and processes—have evolved. Self-publishing has made some aspects easier while introducing its own set of challenges.

I paused my writing career when my daughter was very young; it was a choice to prioritize family, especially during a period of heavy travel. Watching her grow into a driven and accomplished young woman, excelling in college, reignited my passion for writing. Her determination and success provided the spark I needed to take this journey again.

My wife deserves immense gratitude for her patience and understanding during the countless evenings and weekends I spent immersed in this book. As I write this final piece before declaring the book complete, we're already planning a vacation to celebrate—the start of many adventures as we embrace growing older together. I can't wait to explore the world by her side.

On the professional front, I owe profound thanks to our editor, Wendy Raymond Hacker. Who could have imagined that my high school locker buddy would one day be instrumental in crafting this book? Without Wendy, these pages might have been a chaotic mess. Her expertise turned this project into a cohesive and polished work. Wendy, you've been incredible—thank you!

I must also express my gratitude to my co-author, Brandon D'Agostino. Having worked together at four companies, he was my first choice to be a co-author due to his unique blend of business acumen, legal knowledge, and technical ability. Brandon's contributions were invaluable. He authored multiple chapters and provided feedback that elevated my work. I'm grateful for his partnership and look forward to many more years of collaboration.

A special thank you to Doug Austin, editor and primary contributor to eDiscovery Today. I have followed Doug for years, and recently, I have had the chance to work with him and co-present on webinars. Thank you, Doug, for everything you do for the community and for offering us a slice of your time to help.

Finally, a heartfelt thank you to those who've shaped my path and supported me along the way: Peter Kozak, Adam Feher, Peter Parker, Jacob Wild, Kevin Cox, Nicole Thompson, Scott McVeigh, Bob Mill, Amber Johanson, Stephen Stange, Brent Collins, Victor Fiss, and Brad Price. While space doesn't permit me to detail their individual contributions, their influence and encouragement have been vital.

Brandon D'Agostino

My participation in this project was unexpected. One day, John asked me to look at a few chapters of a book he was starting, and over the next few weeks, our conversations about the book went from editing notes to me coming on board as a co-author. I could not be more grateful to him for allowing me to join him on this journey. Writing a book has been a goal of mine for many years, and what better topic for my first one than eDiscovery? It, too, was an unexpected journey for me that began with a phone call from a former manager, Yvonne Rodgers, in July 2008. As I was neck-deep in bar exam preparation, Yvonne called to ask if I would be interested in a newly formed role at BlueCross BlueShield of South Carolina called eDiscovery Counsel. I had to do a quick internet search to figure out what eDiscovery even was (we might have spelled it E-Discovery back then). Fast forward 15 years, and here I am, publishing a book on the topic after having taught it to law students and helped thousands of companies along their eDiscovery journeys. Thank you, Yvonne, for making the phone call that would launch a new career for me.

Several others helped me along the way. First, though, I must thank my wife, Meredith, and my children for always encouraging me to take chances (and dealing with the time commitments those chances bring). They drive me to seek new heights every day.

I also must thank my English teachers and professors from middle school through college. I was very fortunate to have a series of exceptional teachers who nurtured my love of writing, starting with Mrs. Bussey in middle school, Mr. Kaple and Mr. Carter at Summerville High School, and numerous faculty members at the University of South Carolina. Finally, thank you to the amazing staff of the *Charleston Law Review,* who not only started a law journal from scratch in 2007 but demanded excellence as if it had been published for 200 years.

A special thank you to Allyson Haynes Stuart for pitching the idea for a course on eDiscovery back in 2013 and inviting me to co-develop and teach the course with her.

Thank you to Alisa McLellan for her invaluable feedback on early versions of the book. Her insights certainly made the book better in many ways.

Finally, thank you to those colleagues that at critical points in my career offered friendship, guidance, opportunity, and knowledge: Ricky Rowe, Jason Reeve, Krista Jones, Bret Bailine, Patrick O'Hearn, Patrick Murphy, Josh Todd, James Whittington, Josh Williams, Josh Stageburg, Tony Navarro, Anna Simpson, Brooke Seeley, Robert Kreuscher, Patrick Bland, Jacob Wild, Ade Tella, Kiwi Camara, Bob Clemens, Russ Grant, Adam Feher, Peter Kozak, and Peter Parker.

Part I: Information Governance

Chapter 1: The Role of Information Governance in eDiscovery

As a business leader, a legal technologist, or someone with an information technology (IT) focus, you may wonder why information governance (IG) is a dedicated part of this book. Part 1 will focus on IG to provide you with an understanding of why it is part of the eDiscovery reference model (EDRM), and why it is important to understand how IG affects legal workflows.

IG is all about managing your organization's information the right way—from the moment it's created to when it's no longer needed. Think of it as a framework that covers everything: how data is stored, shared, secured, and eventually deleted (in a legally sound way). It's not just about keeping things organized; it's about protecting privacy, meeting compliance requirements, and ensuring data stays accessible and trustworthy.

A well-structured IG program reduces risks and costs associated with eDiscovery by ensuring data is organized, preserved, and easily accessible when legal matters arise. This proactive approach in the early stages of the eDiscovery process allows organizations to manage data more effectively, supporting seamless identification, preservation, and collection of relevant information. IG also aids in compliance and optimizes business operations by streamlining data management practices, leading to better decision-making and reduced litigation costs.

One of the authors (John) has collected sports cards most of his life. He has cards that he collected himself, and, over the years, he's purchased many from other collectors. For years, they were stored in unorganized boxes and totes in his basement. He had an idea of where certain cards were located but wasn't sure. Locating specific cards became a needle-in-a-haystack operation, often consuming hours. During COVID, he organized the entire collection by sport, year, card manufacturer, and even down to the number order of cards. He labeled the outside of each box for convenience. If he needs to find a card now, his effort is a matter of minutes rather than hours of searching where he thinks it *may* be. This is the essence of IG – organizing data to make future work efforts more efficient.

In this chapter, we're setting the stage for everything that comes next. You'll find many definitions and big-picture ideas here, giving you the tools to understand IG and why it matters. Whether it's about keeping your data safe or making your workflows smoother, IG is where it all begins.

Key Themes in This Chapter

- Introduction and Overview of Information Governance
- General Goals of Information Governance
- How Information Governance Plays a Pivotal Role in eDiscovery

Understanding IG

Information Governance (IG) refers to the overarching framework that governs how an organization manages its data throughout its lifecycle, from creation to final disposition. This includes the processes, policies, and standards that guide information collection, storage, use, dissemination, archiving, and destruction.

Organizations face numerous challenges that complicate data management. Employees use various applications across departments, sometimes without IT oversight or approval, leading to shadow IT systems that bypass existing governance frameworks. The rise of hybrid work has introduced challenges to traditional governance, with employees creating, accessing, and sharing sensitive data from diverse locations and devices. These shifts have made it more difficult to maintain consistent oversight of how information is accessed, shared, and stored within an organization.

Organizations increasingly rely on third-party environments to host critical applications, introducing new data security and compliance complexities. As cyber threats become more sophisticated, these complexities are at risk of being exploited, testing the resilience of outdated governance systems. As the regulatory landscape evolves with such laws as General Data Protection Regulation (GDPR), Health Insurance Portability and Accountability Act (HIPAA), California Consumer Privacy Act (CCPA), Financial Industry Regulatory Authority (FINRA), and emerging state, national, and global privacy regulations are introduced, IG platforms must be flexible to guarantee adherence to these regulations. These dynamics highlight the urgent need for comprehensive and updated IG strategies to address data management risks efficiently.

Effective information governance ensures data is managed in compliance with regulatory requirements while also promoting information security, privacy, and operational efficiency. By streamlining the management of data assets, IG allows organizations to reduce risk, improve decision-making, and maximize the value of their information. IG's role in managing information involves various stages:

Creation: The process begins with planning and defining how data will be created and which applications will be used to create it. This step ensures the data is captured accurately and securely to meet operational and legal requirements.

Storage and Maintenance: Proper storage systems ensure data is accessible, secure, and maintained for as long as necessary, based on retention policies. Storage systems must balance accessibility and security.

Use: Data is used for decision-making, operations, or other organizational functions. IG ensures this usage is in line with organizational policies and legal requirements.

Retention: Retention schedules ensure data is kept only as long as necessary for business, compliance, or legal reasons. This prevents data ROT (redundant, obsolete, or trivial data).

Disposition: Once data is no longer needed, it is disposed of securely. This ensures sensitive data is inaccessible after it is no longer required.

An efficient IG framework helps organizations handle data throughout its lifecycle and benefits legal obligations such as preserving information for legal events. This is essential for avoiding penalties, including claims of spoliation (the destruction of evidence, either by negligence or for nefarious reasons). In eDiscovery, litigation costs are often heavy in the processing, hosting, and review phases of an eDiscovery workflow. Thanks to an efficient IG program, significant litigation cost savings can be realized by having fewer, well-preserved documents.

IG ensures the organization can fulfill legal, business, and regulatory requirements, making compliance, data governance, and eDiscovery processes essential.

Goals of Information Governance

IG aims to establish a comprehensive framework that ensures effective, secure, and compliant organizational data management. The key components of this management include:

Data Quality and Integrity: Ensuring data is accurate, consistent, and reliable for decision-making and operational efficiency tasks.

Compliance and Legal Adherence: Enacting practices and policies to adhere to relevant laws, regulations, and industry standards such as GDPR, HIPAA, and others to avoid legal and compliance penalties and ensure ethical data handling.

Data Security and Privacy: Protecting the organization from unauthorized access and breaches and ensuring privacy related to sensitive and personal information through strict security measures.

Efficient Data Management: Ensuring optimal data storage, retrieval, and utilization to align with business processes and strategic objectives.

Accountability

Understanding your organization's roles in managing data will make the discovery process more efficient. During the early eDiscovery tasks, legal personas will interact with various data management team members. There are clearly defined roles and responsibilities in this space. Key roles include:

Data Owners: These individuals or departments are responsible for data quality, security, and compliance for specific data assets.

Data Stewards: These personnel ensure compliance with data policy and standards and focus on data management practices.

Chief Data Officer (CDO): This senior executive role is responsible for the overall data strategy, governance, and management across the organization.

IT and Security Teams: These teams are responsible for implementing and maintaining technical controls and data infrastructure and ensuring data security measures are in place.

Compliance Officers: These personnel monitor data management practices to meet regulatory and legal requirements. They often conduct proactive audits and assessments to ensure compliance while working with external auditors when required.

Due to the nature of IG spanning many areas of the organization, roles and responsibilities are distributed across many individuals and teams, aligning to strengths and ensuring accountability. In many organizations, these roles are not exclusive to one individual. People could hold these roles with different titles across multiple departments in the organization.

Transparency

Transparency is how IG ensures visibility into data usage and handling. It is key to privacy, compliance, and eDiscovery. This is achieved through several mechanisms that allow visibility into how data is managed, accessed, and utilized:

Documentation: Clearly defined policies and procedures outline data management practices, including data creation, storage, access, and disposal.

Data Lineage Tracking: Record maintenance provides information about data origin, movement, and transformation, helping to understand data flows within the organization.

Access Logs and Monitoring: Tracking systems determine who accessed data, when, and for what purpose, ensuring traceability and accountability.

Regular Reporting and Audits: Periodic reviews and reports on data management tasks identify areas of non-compliance and potential improvements to ensure compliance.

Stakeholder Communication: Regularly communication with relevant stakeholders about data policies, changes, and date-related incidents demonstrates trust and transparency.

A good IG practice ensures all data-related activities are transparent and auditable, ensuring trust and accountability within the organization.

Risk Management

IG helps mitigate data-related risks, such as breaches and legal liabilities, by providing the following strategies for identifying and assessing vulnerabilities:

Implement Data Security Measures: Protect data from breaches and unauthorized access by utilizing encryption, access controls, and other security technologies.

Compliance with Regulations: Ensure data handling practices comply with legal and contractual requirements to reduce the risk of penalties and liabilities.

Data Classification and Handling: Mitigate risks associated with varying types of data types by categorizing based on sensitivity and implementing appropriate handling procedures.

Incident Response Plans: Create, implement, and maintain efficient response plans to respond to data breaches or other data-related incidents, minimizing impact and recovery times.

Regular Risk Assessments: Implement proactive measures to address potential data-related risks and conduct ongoing assessments to identify possible gaps.

Training and Awareness Programs: Educate employees about data security, privacy, and governance policies to prevent human errors and insider threats.

IG helps organizations minimize vulnerabilities by proactively addressing these areas before litigation. This ensures data integrity, maintains compliance, and reduces the likelihood and impact of data-related risks.

The Link Between IG and eDiscovery Workflows

IG is a foundational element of effective eDiscovery workflows, yet its impact on legal proceedings is often overlooked. IG's primary role is establishing policies and protocols for proactively managing data, including how it is retained, accessed, shared, and disposed of. This directly impacts the subsequent stages of eDiscovery, such as collection and preservation.

Once the reactive portion of litigation is in motion, eDiscovery workflows seemingly start with identifying relevant data and custodians before moving to preservation and collection. Integrating strong IG practices beforehand ensures organizations are better positioned to manage these tasks efficiently. Proper IG frameworks enable streamlined identification and collection by clarifying data locations, custodians, and applicable policies.

IG is often perceived as an initiative detached from eDiscovery but should be viewed as a critical enabler. Effective IG reduces the risk of non-compliance, spoliation, and over-retention while also improving the speed and accuracy of foundational eDiscovery. By including IG policies in routine operations, organizations can achieve smoother transitions into eDiscovery workflows when legal matters arise.

The Role of Metadata in Information Governance

Metadata plays a key role in implementing effective data governance frameworks. It is a structured descriptor that defines the organization, discovery, management, and data utilization. It typically includes attributes such as the title, author, creation date, modification date, file size, format, and other data lineage. It may also include technical details such as encoding, storage location, access permissions, and relationship between datasets.

This information allows organizations to understand their data, how it flows through the organization, and how it is used. This is important for data management, data security, compliance, and, ultimately, discovery.

Effective metadata management is essential for eDiscovery. Properly managed metadata allows legal teams to locate and identify relevant ESI quickly. During the identification phase of eDiscovery, metadata can be used to filter and search for documents based on key attributes (data ranges, custodians, keywords), streamlining the ECA process. This can significantly reduce downstream review costs and prevent over-preservation of data that does not apply to the matter.

Metadata also benefits the integrity of ESI collection. During the collection phase, metadata can document how data was acquired, ensuring that it is legally defensible and has not been altered. Extracting, maintaining, and reporting the original metadata during eDiscovery is critical to ensuring the data has been handled properly throughout the legal process.

Conclusion

Information Governance (IG) is the foundational framework for managing data throughout its lifecycle, from creation to secure deletion. By establishing robust processes and policies for data collection, storage, usage, retention, and disposal, organizations can ensure compliance with legal and regulatory requirements while promoting data security and operational efficiency. Effective IG helps prevent issues related to data breaches, privacy violations, and non-compliance, which can lead to significant legal and financial consequences.

A proper IG program aids in eDiscovery efforts by reducing legal risk and costs by making identification, preservation, and collection more efficient.

What’s Next

The next chapter will expand on the relationship between IG and its value in foundational eDiscovery. This includes detailed information about how proper IG practices influence eDiscovery, regulatory compliance, and privacy.

Chapter 2: Information Governance Framework from a Legal Perspective

In the last chapter, we discussed the basics of Information Governance. This chapter will detail how a proper Information Governance program provides a framework that will help meet the rigorous demands of legal compliance across your data estate. The legal aspects of IG go beyond data storage and retrieval—they are essential for protecting organizations against penalties, lawsuits, and reputation damage.

Key Themes in This Chapter

- Legal Compliance and Risk Mitigation
- eDiscovery Readiness
- Data Mapping and Lifecycle Management
- Integration of Legal and Business Needs in Information Governance
- Proactive Legal Compliance through IG Audits and Policies

Information Governance as the Foundation for Legal Efficiency

IG is often glossed over when discussing the early stages of eDiscovery with legal professionals. Most legal consultants are guilty of this at times. But, as we mentioned in the previous chapter, it is one of the most important foundational aspects of eDiscovery.

Proper IG management can directly impact how eDiscovery requests are handled. The company can save money by making the remaining eDiscovery workflow steps more efficient.

Well-structured IG policies help reduce the risk of non-compliance with data retention policies (or laws), prevent spoliation, and aid in legal hold and discovery requests. These risks can result in severe legal consequences, such as financial penalties and potential sanctions during litigation.

This is most evident in the early stages of the eDiscovery process, specifically in the identification, preservation, and collection phases. By integrating IG with eDiscovery, organizations can ensure seamless data management, reduce legal risks, and optimize operational efficiency during litigation or regulatory investigations.

Alignment with Business and Legal Needs

Organizations are often mandated to retain specific data for certain periods based on regulations like GDPR, HIPAA, or industry-specific guidelines. These policies must ensure business records remain accessible and defensible for legal matters. At the same time, businesses aim to avoid keeping data longer than necessary, as excessive retention can increase risks such as higher storage costs and making more data available for discovery during litigation.

Involving Stakeholders in IG Policy Development

Multiple groups should be included in planning IG policies to ensure alignment between business and legal units. IT or business departments cannot build a comprehensive and effective IG policy alone. IG practices impact legal and compliance teams, so it only serves the IG team to include business, operations, and legal team members throughout the policy development process.

Legal Team

Legal teams are critical in defining an IG program's compliance requirements. They should provide guidance to ensure data retention, privacy, and legal hold policies align with GDPR, HIPAA, and industry-specific mandates.

This likely includes collaboration with outside counsel to ensure the policies are designed to meet compliance requirements, litigation readiness, and data retention and deletion obligations. With a rapidly changing regulatory landscape and body of case law, in-house counsel should engage outside counsel early and throughout the planning process.

IT and Security

IT and security teams are responsible for implementing the technical infrastructure needed to support IG initiatives. This includes managing data storage, ensuring secure access controls, and deploying encryption protocols. Compliance with privacy laws and other regulations does not only require organizations to keep data accessible for a defined period; it also requires protecting the data from breaches or unauthorized access.

Collaboration with legal teams helps IT understand the specific compliance requirements, while ongoing dialogue with business units ensures these solutions align with operational workflows and do not disrupt productivity.

Business Leaders

Business leaders must be involved in identifying data that is essential for business operations and data that should be prioritized in compliance efforts. Business leaders should also advocate for the necessary resources for compliance and legal teams to do their jobs effectively.

Legal should ensure business units understand an effective IG policy's operational efficiencies and advantages, such as reduced data storage costs, reduced external (or downstream) legal review costs, and better decision-making through enhanced data quality.

Compliance Officers

Compliance officers often liaise among all these teams, overseeing compliance efforts and ensuring they match internal policy and external regulation. They also conduct audits, monitor compliance adherence, and provide feedback to ensure IG strategy remains effective and adaptable to new legal requirements.

Aligning IG policies with legal and business drivers will help compliance officers ensure their organization's data management practices are efficient, cost effective, legally defensible, and compliant with regulatory requirements. This balance is key to maintaining operational efficiency while mitigating risks associated with data breaches, legal disputes, and compliance failures.

For example, a cross-functional working group can create policies for handling data stored in shadow IT systems. This collaboration helps legal teams identify potential risks early and equips IT teams to implement technical solutions that align with legal obligations, such as access controls and retention schedules. Regular communication through regular audits or check-ins ensures alignment as organizational needs evolve.

We've discussed how good IG practices aid in the early stages of an eDiscovery workflow. The remaining portion of the chapter will highlight how IG affects identification, preservation, and collection. This aligns with the remaining parts of the book as we explore each of these steps in the same order in greater detail.

IG's Role in Streamlining Identification

When eDiscovery requests arise, organizations begin by determining if they can respond efficiently. This process starts with investigating what data is accessible and what may be deemed inaccessible due to retention policies or deletion. The following tasks allow for an efficient understanding of their data estate:

Data Mapping and Classification

Data mapping is essential for understanding where data resides within an organization, what retention policies apply to that data, and how data is preserved or deleted. Data mapping aids in the identification phase, which we will explore in greater detail in Part II.

It is important to conduct periodic assessments of data management practices to identify areas of non-compliance, data security weaknesses, and opportunities for improvement. Audits should be an ongoing process to ensure compliance with evolving regulatory standards. An example of this would be conducting regular interviews with business leaders and members of their teams to discover applications or data implemented outside of the IG policy.

IG programs allow organizations to define classification to categorize data based on sensitivity, legal obligations, and business value. By adequately classifying data, organizations can determine how security, retention, and privacy are appropriately managed.

Defensible Deletion and Data Disposition

As data ages and exceeds retention policies, a data expiry program defines how data will be defensibly deleted during its lifecycle. This includes deleting data no longer needed by the business in a way that complies with internal policy or regulatory requirements. Defensible deletion allows organizations to avoid unnecessary storage costs and reduce legal risks by removing ROT data that is not required to be retained. Any data the organization retains is subject to discovery requests and, ultimately, part of the cybersecurity attack surface. A key component of the disposition of this data is proper documentation of the deletion process to demonstrate compliance. When the duty to preserve or produce data arises, any previously deleted data may be scrutinized. Proper documentation mitigates this risk considerably.

Data Minimization and eDiscovery Costs

Another way to limit data collection is through data minimization. This is the practice of limiting data collection, retention, and processing to only what is necessary for a specific legal or operational purpose. Regulations such as GDPR and HIPAA mandate this principle, which requires organizations to collect and retain only the minimum amount of personal data needed for compliance. By adhering to data minimization standards, organizations reduce the risks of penalties for over-collection or over-retention of sensitive data.

Minimizing unnecessary data ensures compliance with privacy laws, lowers storage costs, and makes eDiscovery more efficient. Less irrelevant or redundant data leads to quicker data processing and reduces the volume of information requiring legal review, resulting in significant cost savings since document review is the most expensive phase of the eDiscovery process.

Data minimization enhances data quality by eliminating clutter, ensuring only business-relevant and current information is retained. By minimizing the data in the organization to only essential data, organizations can limit the potential impact of data breaches, as less data is at risk, protecting their reputation and finances. An associated benefit would be reducing eDiscovery costs and reducing the risk that extraneous data gets reviewed or, worse, produced.

Efficient Data Preservation through IG

Efficient legal hold management is one of the most important tasks for minimizing legal risk. All relevant custodians must be informed swiftly and promptly about legal holds, and detailed procedures must be in place to track and confirm communication and compliance.

Beyond the communication portion of a legal hold, all relevant data must be preserved, and automatic deletion policies must be suspended to ensure data is not altered during the hold period. Failure to preserve this data may result in penalties and sanctions.

Consider an organization that uses a sophisticated IG framework to automate the issuance and management of legal holds. Upon receiving a legal hold instruction, the system automatically suspends data deletion for specific categories and custodians, preserving relevant data for litigation while ensuring non-relevant data continues to follow its regular lifecycle. This capability reduces the risk of penalties and ensures eDiscovery processes run smoothly, as the preserved data is readily accessible when needed.

Retention Policies

Organizations must adhere to data retention policies to balance legal and operational demands effectively. Regulated industries face specific mandates under frameworks like GDPR, HIPAA, and SEC 17a-4, while non-regulated sectors define internal policies. These policies ensure critical data remains accessible for legal matters while minimizing risks of over-retention (which increases costs and litigation exposure), or under-retention (which could lead to data loss and penalties).

Lifecycle management aligns legal obligations and business goals by enabling proper retention periods and secure data disposition. This approach reduces the volume of data for eDiscovery and safeguards against legal risks, ensuring readiness for litigation or regulatory reviews.

Ensuring Data Integrity

IG policies are crucial in safeguarding data integrity, ensuring ESI remains unaltered and authentic throughout its lifecycle. Data integrity is vital in litigation because courts and parties to litigation demand accuracy and authenticity of evidence. Robust IG frameworks include encryption, access controls, and version control to protect data from unauthorized changes. By maintaining detailed records of how data is created, stored, accessed, and modified, IG frameworks help establish a chain of custody, ensuring data presented in legal proceedings can be trusted.

From an eDiscovery perspective, preserving the integrity of ESI is a legal obligation, particularly when legal holds are in place. IG policies ensure data can be preserved in its original form and free from tampering in eDiscovery, which is critical for avoiding penalties. An effective IG policy also ensures metadata is preserved along with the data, maintaining crucial information about when, how, and by whom the data was accessed or modified. This helps to demonstrate authenticity and prevent disputes about the accuracy or legitimacy of the evidence presented in litigation.

Enhancing Data Collection with IG

During collection, IG enhances defensibility by enabling controlled, documented, and secure retrieval of ESI. IG policies typically incorporate protocols facilitating secure data collection, ensuring chain-of-custody is maintained, and data integrity is preserved. This makes it easier for organizations to comply with legal and regulatory standards, reducing the costs associated with manual collection and ensuring data is collected efficiently and accurately.

Maintaining Proper Chain of Custody

Another key component of the collection phase is maintaining a proper chain of custody. The chain of custody refers to the documented process that tracks the handling, access, and transfer of data from its original location as used in the ordinary course of business through its collection and ultimate production or presentation in a matter. A clear, unbroken chain provides strong evidence that the data has not been altered or tampered with.

IG plays a crucial role in upholding the chain of custody during collection by establishing protocols and systems that ensure data is handled securely and complies with legal standards. IG frameworks enable organizations to implement automated logging tools, enforce secure transfer methods, and maintain detailed audit trails of all data interactions. By integrating these practices, IG ensures data collected for eDiscovery remains authentic, traceable, and defensible, reducing the risks of spoliation or disputes over data integrity.

Getting Started and Quick Wins

At the end of each part of this book, we will summarize the steps you can take to get started on your eDiscovery journey, along with some "quick wins" that will accelerate your success.

For the summary of Part 1 of the book, we will focus on how you can work with your information governance teams to lay the groundwork for a successful foundational eDiscovery workflow.

We provide practical steps to establish a strong foundation for information governance (IG) and highlight immediate actions (quick wins) to accelerate success. These strategies are designed to improve eDiscovery readiness, compliance, and overall data management efficiency.

Engage Cross-Functional Teams

Ensure legal has a presence in cross-functional teams with IT, compliance, and business units. Make sure policies comprehensively address operational and regulatory needs. This collaboration enhances alignment with organizational goals.

Assess Current Practices

Conduct an inventory of data handling practices, focusing on data creation, storage, access, and deletion. Identify gaps in compliance and transparency that could lead to legal risks.

Define and Document Policies

Validate policies for data retention, deletion, access, and security. Ensure they align with legal mandates like GDPR, HIPAA, and other relevant regulations. Use these policies to establish a baseline for legal efforts.

Prioritize High-Risk Data

Focus on datasets with the highest regulatory or business impact, such as customer information, financial records, and sensitive employee data. Addressing these areas first provides immediate benefits and reduces risk.

If not previously completed, extend policies to ephemeral messaging. Define retention and deletion policies for platforms like WhatsApp or Signal to prevent data loss during litigation.

Work with IT to integrate third-party systems, such as external SaaS platforms, to centralize IG systems for visibility and control.

Educate and Train Staff

Launch awareness campaigns and/or conduct training sessions to ensure all data management employees understand their roles in IG and legal collaboration, particularly in legal, compliance, and data security areas.

Host legal hold workshops to educate IT and compliance staff on legal holds and how they may affect information governance and data management.

Implement Simple Tools and Processes

Start small by piloting automated tools for legal holds, data classification, or access monitoring. These can streamline early IG and legal initiatives and provide measurable results quickly.

Policy Rollouts

Publish and distribute data retention and access policies. Highlight their importance in reducing risks and improving compliance. These policies are easy to implement and offer immediate visibility.

> **Example:** A financial services firm implemented a standardized data retention policy across all departments, ensuring compliance with industry regulations like GDPR and FINRA. The rollout included guidelines for retaining customer financial data for seven years and provided templates for each department to adapt the policy to their workflows. Within two months, this effort reduced non-compliant data storage practices by 30%.

Activate Access Logs and Monitoring

Enable existing system features to log data access and usage. Review logs regularly to establish traceability and detect potential issues.

> **Example:** A global corporation under a litigation hold enabled access logging across its document management system. The legal team used these logs to monitor access to ESI (electronically stored information) under preservation. When discrepancies surfaced, such as unauthorized deletions or unusual access patterns, the logs provided critical evidence to support compliance during the meet-and-confer. By addressing these issues promptly, the company avoided spoliation claims and sanctions, while demonstrating defensible processes to the court, enhancing its overall litigation posture.

Begin Data Mapping and Classification

Identify and document where critical data resides, its retention requirements, and how it flows through the organization. This foundational activity supports compliance and eDiscovery readiness.

Use visualization software tools to map connections between custodians and data repositories to view potential ESI sources comprehensively. Pay special attention to mapping efforts on collaborative platforms such as Teams, Slack, and shared cloud file repositories, which often hold critical yet overlooked data.

> **Example:** A financial services company initiated a data mapping project to prepare for an anticipated regulatory investigation. Using specialized software, the legal and IT teams identified and documented ESI across cloud storage, email archives, and chat platforms like Teams. The tool also linked custodians to datasets, revealing that archived emails contained critical discussions relevant to the investigation. The company ensured compliance with legal hold requirements and regulatory standards by integrating retention schedules into the mapping process. This streamlined discovery reduced the preservation scope by 35% and avoided overcollection of non-relevant data.

Launch Defensible Deletion Programs

Safely eliminate redundant, obsolete, and trivial (ROT) data while documenting the deletion process to ensure compliance. This reduces storage costs and mitigates unnecessary eDiscovery risks.

> **Example:** A multinational financial institution implemented a defensible deletion program in preparation for anticipated litigation. Leveraging automated classification tools, the legal and compliance teams identified and eliminated 15 TB of ROT data from email archives and shared drives. The deletion was executed under documented retention schedules and a legal hold protocol to ensure compliance

> with regulatory and litigation hold requirements. This proactive effort reduced the data volume subject to eDiscovery by 40%, streamlining the identification and review phases and saving the company $500,000 in legal costs during the first case alone.

Establish Legal Hold Protocols

Implement a straightforward legal hold process that includes data management for custodian data sets and automated notifications and tracking of legal holds to ensure compliance. This prevents spoliation and demonstrates IG's impact on legal readiness.

> **Example:** A technology company enhanced its eDiscovery readiness by integrating a data mapping and classification tool into its legal hold workflow. Upon triggering a legal hold, the tool automatically identified relevant data repositories based on predefined criteria, such as email servers, cloud storage, and shared drives. The system issued tailored hold notices and tracked responses. This integration streamlined custodian identification and ensured that high-value datasets were secured within hours, reducing spoliation risks and demonstrating defensible processes during litigation.

Quick Reporting and Transparency

Create simple dashboards or reports to showcase metrics like reduced storage costs, improved compliance rates, or access control findings. Use these to communicate early wins to stakeholders.

> **Example:** A global corporation created a dashboard to monitor IG metrics, such as storage costs and legal hold compliance rates. One report showed a 15% reduction in

ROT data within six months, which was presented to stakeholders to demonstrate IG's impact on operational efficiency and litigation readiness.

Conduct an Initial Audit

Perform a fundamental review of compliance adherence and highlight any gaps. This assessment will establish a culture of accountability and prepare the organization for regulatory or legal scrutiny.

> **Example:** A financial services firm conducted a comprehensive data mapping audit for its eDiscovery readiness initiative. The audit revealed several previously undocumented data repositories, including cloud-based collaboration tools used by multiple departments. These tools contained potentially relevant ESI for an anticipated class action lawsuit. By integrating these data sources into its eDiscovery processes and updating its legal hold workflows, the firm ensured complete compliance, streamlined its data collection efforts, and mitigated the risk of missing critical evidence, which could have resulted in sanctions during litigation.

Streamline High-Risk Data Workflows

Focus on high-value, high-risk datasets to address immediate legal or compliance risks. Ensure they are securely stored, easily accessible, and compliant with retention policies.

> **Example:** A corporation facing antitrust litigation identified email communications and contracts from key custodians as high-risk data. Using a data mapping tool, the legal team created a comprehensive map of repositories containing

potentially relevant ESI. The team classified data based on relevance and sensitivity, tagging high-priority datasets for immediate legal hold. This approach ensured compliance with legal obligations and reduced document review costs by 40% by streamlining the eDiscovery process and focusing review efforts on the most critical data.

Conclusion

Poor data governance can lead to significant legal and financial consequences. By integrating IG practices with eDiscovery, organizations can streamline legal responses, reduce operational costs, and minimize risks. The proactive nature of IG ensures data is well-organized, easily identified, preserved, and collected in a defensible and compliant manner. In contrast, a lack of integration between IG and eDiscovery can lead to costly delays, compliance failures, fines, and penalties. Therefore, a strong IG framework is a business necessity and a critical component of litigation and compliance readiness.

Data breaches resulting from weak access controls or inadequate encryption can lead to litigation, government investigations, and penalties, especially in industries handling sensitive data like healthcare or financial services. Recent changes to SEC rules require all publicly traded companies to disclose security breaches, and recent enforcement actions indicate that companies and individuals can be held responsible for inadequate security controls. Regulatory bodies, such as those enforcing GDPR or HIPAA, impose heavy fines for noncompliance with data protection laws. A structured IG framework is necessary to reduce exposure to these risks.

What's Next

Building on the foundation of information governance (IG), the next chapter will focus on identifying electronically stored information (ESI), a crucial step in the eDiscovery process. Identification involves locating potential sources of relevant ESI, understanding its context within the organization, and assessing its accessibility for legal or regulatory needs.

Chapter 3 will address the following key topics related to identification:

Mapping ESI Sources: Techniques for pinpointing the location of relevant ESI storage, including on-premises systems, cloud environments, mobile devices, and ephemeral messaging platforms.

Custodian Identification: Methods for identifying key individuals responsible for or connected to relevant data, enhancing the precision of the identification process.

Data Mapping Tools: Leveraging technology to create and maintain comprehensive data maps that streamline the identification of ESI.

Cross-Functional Collaboration: Strategies for coordinating between IT, legal, and compliance teams to ensure all relevant ESI is accounted for without duplicative efforts.

The next chapter provides actionable insights to establish efficient and defensible practices for identifying ESI, laying the groundwork for its preservation and subsequent stages of eDiscovery.

Part II – Identification

Chapter 3 – The Role of Identification in eDiscovery

Part II of the book focuses on identification in eDiscovery. Identification is essential to eDiscovery, ensuring proper scoping for preservation and allowing legal professionals to begin early case assessment (ECA) by understanding the data involved in the matter and the custodians.

Key Themes in This Chapter

- Introduction to Identification
- Custodian and Data Mapping
- Compliance and Risk Considerations
- Risk Mitigation through Proper Identification

Introduction to Identification

In the previous section, we highlighted how information governance is the foundation of an efficient eDiscovery workflow, focusing on proactive efforts to improve the discovery process.

The identification phase is the foundation of the reactive portion and typically the first phase of any eDiscovery project. Identification is essential for locating potential sources of ESI that may be relevant to the matter and for determining the scope, breadth, and depth of data that needs to be preserved and collected for downstream eDiscovery phases.

Most texts focus on data in the identification stage. Identifying relevant data sources is a priority of the identification stage, but we would argue that custodian identification and management play an equally important role. To properly understand the data involved in a matter, identification must include the ability to review custodians *and* data to get a complete view of proper data relevance.

Most of this is captured via questionnaires or live interviews during the legal hold process. However, mistakes can happen during these manual processes. The following section discusses why data mapping is a vital identification component. We also introduce the concept of custodian mapping, which is equally vital to legal teams as they try to understand who is relevant to the case. This is the critical link between the defined custodians, potential custodians, or people of interest and their data.

> For example, an organization's legal team begins working on a matter involving a software product released four years ago. As the product succeeded in the market, a competitor has alleged infringement of their intellectual property. The legal team launched an investigation into the development group; however, as the company has grown, the team has changed a lot since the original release. Understanding where the data is located is one aspect, but how does the legal team determine who was on the team at the time of feature releases? Who was the team's manager, and who were the team members? Is anyone from that team still with the company but in a different role? Identification is a bit like going back in time to reconstruct the state of the organization in terms of both people and systems during the relevant time of the matter.

Early Case Assessment (ECA) also ties directly to effective identification, allowing quicker evaluation of a case's merits based on the identified data relevant to the identified custodians. Think of this beyond simple data mapping, but as an effective mapping of the proper custodians to the appropriate data.

Steps to Effective Identification

Effective identification involves many components. This includes understanding data repositories such as email servers, cloud storage, social media, databases, etc., and identifying the custodians who created, accessed, or managed potentially relevant data in those repositories. Precise identification helps manage the scope of the discovery, avoiding over-preservation (which can inflate costs) or under-preservation (which can result in sanctions).

Determining Scope

Identification begins with defining an initial scope. Best practice is to form a cross-functional team of legal counsel, litigation support professionals, a project manager, and IT experts at the outset of a matter. This team should discuss the data repositories that may be in scope and any risks associated with those repositories, such as potential collection or preservation challenges and/or regulatory impacts.

In litigation, the parties to a case are required by FRCP 26(f) [2] to meet and confer to discuss the scope of discovery, including preservation and production of ESI. The minimum output of this conference is a scheduling order submitted to the court (and becomes part of the case record once approved by the judge). An ESI protocol provides a more detailed list of everything the parties agreed to during the conference related to eDiscovery. We discuss

---

[2] Fed. R. Civ. P. 26(f). *See* Fed. R. Civ. P. 26(f)(3)(Providing the minimum elements required for a discovery plan).

the ESI protocol in a later chapter. Sound IG policies and thorough identification of custodians and relevant data sources equip each party's counsel to accurately represent their client's capabilities and avoid commitments that are either impossible or very expensive for their client.

The Rule 26(f) Conference, or "meet and confer" as it is commonly called, must occur a minimum of 21 days before the Scheduling Order is due to the Court. The Scheduling Order is due no later than 120 days after the complaint is served on the defendant. Therefore, the 26(f) conference must occur no later than 99 days after the complaint is served on the defendant. That period will fly by; taking action very quickly after litigation commences ensures each party is prepared for this important milestone that sets the tone for the case.

Identifying Custodians

Historically, custodian identification has been performed by some combination of meetings with HR and business leaders, looking at org charts, viewing permissions or sharing settings in relevant data repositories, input from outside counsel, analyzing prior litigation, and live interviews with key custodians. Many organizations still perform custodian identification this way, and there is nothing inherently wrong with this approach. Through diligent efforts, counsel can use a "no stone unturned" approach that often leads to over-preservation but helps avoid potential sanctions.

Proactive custodian management, reporting, and tracking are key to making this portion of the process more efficient. Direct engagement with custodians is still required, but if you go into that portion of the process with a key understanding of the custodian landscape, you can make the identification process more efficient with less risk.

A custodian management system provides an excellent basis for the early part of the identification process. Custodian management systems, such as Cloudficient CaseFusion:Identify, provide the following benefits:

- Connect to Human Resources Information Systems (HRIS) to understand who custodians are and to whom they report. Provide a history of their organizational engagement, tracking departmental changes, name changes, responsibilities, managers or direct reports, etc.
- Allow for merging of legacy HRIS and directories from acquired companies, making identification easier when matters involve the acquired companies' employees

Creating a Custodian Map

The custodian map is a new concept that streamlines the historically manual process of identifying data sources for each custodian. This automated process bridges the gap between the selected custodians and the data map. Like the introduction of custodian management efforts, the custodian map is a new technique that shows how the custodians interacted with data sources in the data map and reduces the risk of potentially missing important data sources.

The custodian management system already understands the custodian and (potentially) the applications the custodian uses. Tying this to the data map is the next logical step, making the custodian interview process more of a review than a fact-finding mission.

We will cover custodian mapping in more detail in Chapter 4.

Engaging With Custodians

After reviewing the initial custodian list to determine what apps are in use and where relevant data is likely stored, the legal team should engage with the custodian directly by conducting interviews with individuals most likely to control or create relevant data or those who were directly involved in the events leading to the litigation. These interviews help legal teams understand the custodian's role in managing the ESI and provide insight into potential locations of relevant data. If the organization does not have a custodian management solution, interviews are the primary way to identify additional data sources and custodians. If the organization does have a custodian management solution, this process validates the information gathered from that system and could potentially uncover gaps in the information-gathering stage. All engagement with custodians – both interviews and correspondence should be documented.

In these interactions, custodians can provide a broad understanding of the tools, platforms, and practices used to manage relevant ESI, such as the types of data they use, the locations where data is stored, and their data-sharing methods. Additionally, discussing security measures, retention practices, and any legacy or third-party systems they use ensures all relevant data sources are considered. These interviews also allow the legal team to ensure custodians understand their preservation obligations, particularly in legal holds.

Many of these steps are discussed further in the next chapter, exploring the custodian interview process, specific questions to ask, and a deeper dive into data sources. This overview provides the framework for understanding how crucial custodian engagement is to the identification process and how it helps create a streamlined, defensible discovery effort.

Understanding Data Sources

Based on the information uncovered from the custodian review, the next step is understanding the various data sources where the custodians work. In the past, this was mostly limited to email and unstructured file data. Legal teams must now consider these traditional data sources, along with messaging and collaboration applications, cloud-based services, social media, and mobile devices.

Each data source may have different storage, retention, search, and export methods. Modern eDiscovery requires a keen understanding of how these tasks are accomplished in various environments.

Preservation and collection are also affected, so we explore each in its respective chapters and introduce potential solutions to this management challenge.

Addressing Legacy Systems and Archived Data

It is essential to consider historical and archived data to fully capture the scope of potentially relevant data. Custodians who interact with legacy systems or archived data might have access to information pertinent to the case, though it might be stored in systems difficult to access or with limited export options. If custodians are aware of lost or deleted data (or even legacy systems that were retired), forensic recovery and restoring backups can be investigated. Just because data is archived or only exists on backup media, it is not excluded from eDiscovery.

Engagement with Third-Party Systems

Legal teams should examine interactions with third-party vendors, who may hold additional data pertinent to the case. Identifying any third-party systems accessed by custodians allows for a more thorough understanding of data storage locations and compliance with vendor-related agreements that might impact eDiscovery.

Creating a Data Map

As you understand in-scope data sources, create (or update) your data map. A well-maintained data map is a strategic tool that helps locate where data resides, its types, and its flow into, throughout, and out of the organization.

This map includes structured and unstructured data, helping avoid missteps during identification and streamlining preservation and collection efforts. Data mapping facilitates a deeper understanding of legal and business needs, ensuring teams do not overreach or under-collect. Much of your data mapping efforts will be done with the help of information governance teams, as discussed in Part I

The data map includes mapping the organization's network systems (servers, cloud storage, databases) and devices (desktops, mobile phones, external storage) to ensure no potential ESI is overlooked. Cloud and hybrid environments should also be part of the mapping process.

The data map should also include details about the ESI stored across the organization's systems, including structured (databases) and unstructured (emails, file servers) data. The map is a centralized, living document integrating information from eDiscovery efforts and custodians. Noting data sources unique to specific business units ensures the legal team can react quickly to preserve evidence when custodians from those business units are identified in future litigation.

Scope of the Data

The scope of data must be defined by determining its breadth (different sources or types of ESI), depth (how far back to look), and volume (how much data needs to be preserved and collected). Defining this scope at the identification stage ensures only relevant data is considered, reducing the risk of overcollection.

Compliance and Risk Considerations

During the identification process, it is important to understand and properly manage risks to data subject to data protection laws, like the GDPR and HIPAA. These regulations mandate strict oversight of sensitive data, and failure to identify data correctly can lead to non-compliance, resulting in fines, sanctions, and/or reputational damage. Identifying applicable data handling protocols ensures compliance, and if necessary, to shield the organization from discovery penalties, counsel can propose a protective order or prescribe special handling protocols for sensitive data.

Omitting key data or failing to properly limit scope during identification can lead to severe consequences, including increased costs from reviewing irrelevant data or, worse, the loss of critical information that could affect case outcomes through sanctions, increased costs, or even dismissal. Legal teams should emphasize precision in this phase to mitigate these risks. This is also a case for proactively utilizing your organization's custodian management and mapping tools.

Key Compliance Risks:

- **Overlooking Sensitive Data:** During identification, missing key data sources or failing to recognize sensitive data can result in noncompliance with regulations.
- **Cross-Border Data Transfers:** Identifying where data resides is crucial in international cases, as data sovereignty laws may restrict where data can be transferred or processed.
- **Inadequate Documentation:** Maintaining accurate documentation throughout the identification phase is essential for demonstrating compliance and ensuring data integrity. Failure to do so could lead to compliance audits and penalties.

In the next chapter, we discuss ways to mitigate these risks.

Security and Access Control

Finally, review security controls to understand how custodians manage access to their data based on organizational or contractual requirements. This ensures data is preserved and handled appropriately and protected from unauthorized access, protecting both the data and the business from additional risk during eDiscovery.

By systematically engaging with custodians and leveraging comprehensive mapping techniques, legal teams enhance their ability to identify and preserve relevant ESI, facilitating a thorough and defensible eDiscovery process.

Challenges in Data Identification

Data identification during eDiscovery presents several challenges that can complicate the process. Some of the most common challenges are:

Fragmented Data Sources: Modern organizations store data across various platforms, such as email servers, cloud storage, collaboration tools, and social media. Identifying relevant data from these dispersed systems can be difficult, especially when some systems lack robust search capabilities.

Unstructured Data: Much of the data that needs to be identified is unstructured (e.g., chat messages, emails, documents), making it harder to sift through than structured databases. Legacy systems designed for specific types of data, like email, may not effectively accommodate newer forms of communication, further complicating the identification process.

Custodian Identification: Finding data is not enough; identifying the correct custodians (individuals who own or handle relevant data) is crucial. Custodian mapping can be complex when employees change roles or leave organizations. Failure to correctly identify custodians can lead to gaps in data collection.

Over-Identification and Under-Identification Risks: The eDiscovery process becomes more expensive and time-consuming if too much irrelevant data is identified. Conversely, under-identification, where relevant data is missed, can lead to noncompliance or legal penalties. Proper scoping and collaboration between legal and IT teams are essential to avoid these pitfalls.

Data Privacy and Compliance: Identifying data subject to privacy laws and other regulations is a significant challenge. Legal teams must ensure they don't inadvertently violate these regulations while producing relevant information in eDiscovery.

Legacy Systems: Older systems often lack efficient search or indexing capabilities, making extracting and identifying relevant data difficult. This can result in delays or require costly workarounds to obtain the necessary information.

These challenges highlight the complexity of data identification, which requires a strategic approach and collaboration across multiple departments to mitigate risks and ensure compliance.

Conclusion

In this chapter, we reviewed the critical role of identification in the eDiscovery process. As the first reactive phase in an eDiscovery workflow, identification is pivotal in locating relevant electronically stored information (ESI) and determining the scope of the data that must be preserved and collected. The chapter emphasized the importance of identifying data sources and understanding custodians who manage or interact with the data. Techniques like custodian interviews, data mapping, and custodian mapping were introduced to streamline this process.

The chapter outlined the key steps to effective identification, beginning with pre-identification tasks such as meet-and-confer sessions and risk assessments. It further highlighted the significance of balancing the breadth, depth, and volume of data being identified to avoid unnecessary costs and ensure compliance with regulatory obligations like GDPR and HIPAA. The goal is to create an efficient, defensible identification process that supports downstream activities in the workflow while minimizing the risk of errors, sanctions, or costly missteps.

What's Next

Chapter 4 dives into the tools and techniques that streamline the identification process and bridge process gaps between legal and IT teams. We highlight practical strategies for custodian mapping, conducting effective interviews, and leveraging technology like APIs and connectors to locate relevant data efficiently. Readers will gain actionable insights into implementing systems and workflows that enhance accuracy and speed during eDiscovery while reducing risks and improving team collaboration.

Chapter 4 – Tools and Techniques for Efficient Identification

This chapter discusses practical strategies and technologies that enhance the eDiscovery identification process, providing actionable steps to bridge the gap between legal and IT teams. By leveraging these methods, legal teams can improve the accuracy and speed with which they identify relevant electronically stored information (ESI).

Key Themes in This Chapter

- Practical Strategies for Enhancing eDiscovery Identification Processes
- The Role of Custodian Mapping in Linking Individuals to Relevant Data
- Effective Techniques for Conducting and Leveraging Custodian Interviews
- Comprehensive Data Mapping to Locate and Manage ESI Sources
- Integration of Third-party Systems Using APIs and Connectors to Streamline Workflow

Custodian Mapping

Custodian mapping adds value to the identification stage of eDiscovery by revealing employees' past departments, teams, direct managers, direct reports, and other information that can enhance the legal team's understanding of data ownership and potential relevance to cases.

After reviewing the custodian mapping information, the legal team should engage with the custodian directly by conducting interviews with individuals most likely to control or create relevant data. These interviews help legal teams understand the custodian's involvement in the case and their role in managing the ESI and provide insight into potential locations of relevant data.

Manual Custodian Mapping

Without dedicated custodian management software, managing custodians during the identification phase of eDiscovery requires meticulous manual effort. These activities, collectively known as "custodian mapping," are crucial for understanding custodial relationships and data ownership, which are fundamental to the legal matter.

Identifying Key Custodians

The first step in custodian mapping involves identifying key custodians likely to possess or control relevant data. This is achieved by conducting interviews to determine their roles, responsibilities, and data management practices. Additionally, legal teams must assess the custodians' involvement in the case, including their historical roles, which might reveal critical insights into their connection to relevant data.

Mapping Custodians' Electronic Identities

Custodians are using more applications than ever before, and each system may identify the custodian using a different unique identifier. While their corporate email address is the most likely identifier used by corporate systems, custodians may have created accounts using their personal email address or some other username not associated with their primary corporate ID. These additional identifiers should be noted during custodian interviews.

Any custodian- or department-specific system should be investigated further to gather information needed for preservation and collection.

Documenting Custodial Relationships

Understanding and documenting custodial relationships is another vital aspect of custodian mapping. This includes creating records of custodians' past and current affiliations within various departments, teams, and management hierarchies. Changes such as promotions, transfers, or terminations are also essential, as these transitions can significantly affect data ownership and accessibility.

Reviewing Custodial Data Practices

These practices align with data mapping, which is discussed in greater detail in the information governance chapters of this book. As you work through a matter and determine data sources for custodians, a comprehensive tracing of data sources can help validate custodian mapping. This involves identifying all locations where a custodian's data may reside, including personal devices, network drives, cloud platforms, or proprietary systems.

In addition to knowing where custodians' data resides, reviewing how they handle data provides deeper insights into data relevance and risk. This includes exploring how they share data, retention practices, and any use of external storage platforms. Evaluating compliance with established retention policies is equally important to uncover potential risks, such as reliance on personal backups, which could complicate legal hold or preservation efforts.

Mitigating Risks

Risk mitigation is integral to the process when custodian mapping is performed manually. Addressing gaps or inaccuracies in collected information involves iterative interviews and cross-referencing findings against the data map. Collaboration with cross-functional teams, including IT and compliance, is essential to validating data and ensuring comprehensive coverage of all custodians and their information going forward.

Custodian Mapping Tools

While custodian mapping can be accomplished without specialized software, the process is inherently labor-intensive and susceptible to human error. Implementing custodian management tools can significantly enhance efficiency and accuracy by automating data tracking, centralizing reporting, and streamlining the overall workflow, ultimately supporting a more robust eDiscovery process.

Custodian mapping solutions are currently in their infancy. Solutions like Cloudficient CaseFusion:Identify connect to HRIS systems and other business systems to automate most of the steps in the "manual custodian mapping" section above.

Custodian mapping solutions can monitor and track identities, recording custodial relationships over time to provide key information during the early stages of identification. These tools can reduce the required steps and time spent in custodian interviews to uncover this information.

Custodian Interviews

Custodian interviews are vital to the identification process. They fill information gaps, clarify the custodians' roles, and support legal holds.

When an organization lacks a custodian management solution, custodian interviews become the primary method to initiate the identification process. These interviews are crucial in gathering the necessary information to start the identification. However, these interviews are essential even when a custodian management solution is in place. They validate the information collected from the system and can potentially uncover gaps in the information-gathering stage, ensuring a comprehensive identification process. A custodian management solution can provide a streamlined process for these interviews, as well as a secure place to store the information learned and link it to other information in the matter.

Interviews with custodians should cover various topics to build a clear understanding of data and its relevance. Custodian interviews typically span two areas in the eDiscovery workflow. In the identification stage, essential information is gathered to determine information about the custodians, their data sets, and applications in use. This helps set the stage for the remaining workflow and provides valuable information during the preservation and collection stages. Interviews during the preservation stage determine what data is placed on legal hold, what information is delivered to the custodian about their duty to preserve, etc. More information is provided in the preservation chapters of this book.

Custodian Interview Goals

Custodian interviews should explore data creation and storage practices, including the types of data (emails, spreadsheets, contracts) they produce and storage locations (personal devices, shared drives, cloud platforms).

They should validate or expand any information already received during the identification process. Interview topics could consist of:

- Reviewing custodians' hardware, software, and communication tools, such as laptops, mobile devices, applications used for business (e.g., Outlook, Teams, Slack, Salesforce, Signal, iMessage), helps pinpoint additional repositories of electronically stored information (ESI).
- Identifying personal devices and external platforms like Dropbox or OneDrive further clarifies potential data locations and sharing practices, which is critical for tracing internal and external communications.
- Analyzing data-sharing behaviors and retention practices offers insight into potential copies of ESI across organizational and third-party systems. Legal teams must assess whether custodians adhere to retention policies or rely on personal backups, making preservation and collection potentially more challenging.

Custodian Interview Topics

The custodian interview process typically includes many or all the following topics.

Role and Responsibilities

Job Function: The custodian's job function helps clarify the data types they generate or manage. For example, a custodian in a financial role might handle transactional data, while someone in HR may have access to employee records.

Involvement in the Case: Discuss the custodian's direct or indirect involvement in the matter, which can influence what data sources must be preserved.

Other Custodians Involved

It is best practice always to ask custodians who collaborated with them or who else may have created relevant data. Even with advanced custodian management platforms, you cannot always predict the complete list of custodians for a complex matter.

Data Creation and Storage Habits

Types of Data Created: Determine the types of data the custodian creates, such as emails, reports, spreadsheets, contracts, or databases.

Storage Locations: Identify where this data is stored, whether on personal devices, shared network drives, cloud platforms (e.g., Dropbox, OneDrive, Google Drive), or proprietary systems like document management platforms.

Hardware: Review all devices the custodian uses to access or store data, including laptops, desktops, mobile phones, tablets, or external hard drives. IT should note any personally owned devices used for work purposes.

Software: Discuss the software and applications the custodian uses, such as email clients (e.g., Outlook), collaboration tools (e.g., Slack, Microsoft Teams), project management systems (e.g., Jira, Trello), and financial or CRM systems. This helps identify where ESI may be located.

Communications Platforms

Email and Messaging Systems: Confirm which email systems and messaging platforms the custodian uses, including any non-company platforms (e.g., Outlook, Teams, Slack, Salesforce, Signal, iMessage) used for business communication.

Collaboration Tools: Review any use of tools like Microsoft Teams, Slack, or Zoom and how files are shared or stored within these systems. Were meetings recorded, and are those recordings still available?

File and Data Sharing

Internal and External Sharing: Discuss how the custodian shares files with others within and outside the organization. This includes understanding third-party services or tools they use for file sharing (e.g., OneDrive, Dropbox). Are collaboration tools like Slack and Teams used to communicate and share files with external parties?

Shared Drives and Databases: Identify any shared network drives, file shares, or databases the custodian uses regularly. This helps you understand where other ESI or additional versions of ESI may reside.

Legacy Systems and Archived Data: Determine if the custodian has access to older systems no longer used to store new data, historical data, or archived materials that might still be relevant to the case.

Deleted or Lost Data: Inquire whether the custodian knows any data that may have been deleted or otherwise lost and whether recovery is possible through backups or forensic recovery.

Third-Party Systems

Vendors and Partners: Identify any third-party vendors or systems that may hold relevant data. These could involve cloud services or outsourced services containing critical information and require third-party support to retrieve the data. Knowing this as early as possible can help avoid delays later.

Custodian Interview Process

Once all interview topics are determined, the next step is to start the interview process.

Pre-Interview Preparation

Understand the Case: Before interviewing custodians, thoroughly understand the nature of the case, including the legal issues, timelines, and key individuals. Familiarize yourself with relevant documents, events, and any previous discovery efforts.

Identify Custodians: Collaborate with legal and IT teams to identify key custodians. These are individuals likely to possess or control relevant information, such as emails, files, or communications.

Gather Custodian Information: Obtain preliminary information on each custodian's role, responsibilities, and possible data sources they control (e.g., email accounts, cloud storage, devices).

Prepare a Customized Questionnaire: Tailor your questions to the case's specifics, focusing on the custodian's involvement in the matter, the data sources they use, and their document handling practices.

Initial Custodian Outreach

Send Interview Notices: Notify custodians about the eDiscovery process and schedule interviews. Provide information about the purpose of the interview, their role in the case, and the importance of preserving relevant data.

Legal Hold Notice: Ensure custodians have received and acknowledged the legal hold notice, explaining their obligation to preserve relevant information and avoid data spoliation. This notice also provides an overview of the case and help prepare them for the interview. More information is provided on legal hold notices in the chapters on preservation.

Conducting the Custodian Interview

Explain the Process: Begin the interview by explaining the purpose of the interview and the custodian's role in the eDiscovery process. Reiterate the importance of preserving data.

Ask About Roles and Responsibilities: Confirm the custodian's role in the organization and how their job relates to the matter. This helps frame the types of data they might possess.

Identify Data Sources: Ask about all locations where relevant data may exist (e.g., email, shared drives, personal devices, third-party applications like Slack or Teams).

Inquire about any tools, software, or databases they use for communication or project management.

Confirm whether they use collaboration tools that share links instead of files and understand how they manage modern attachments or shared documents.

Explain and emphasize the organization's commitment to privacy if personal devices are in scope.

Document Review: Ask whether they have relevant paper or physical documents. Many discovery processes focus on electronic data, but physical records may also need to be considered.

Determine Custodian Communication Channels: Identify all relevant communication channels (email, messaging apps, etc.) the custodian uses regularly and may contain pertinent information.

Follow-up Questions Based on Specifics

Project-Specific Questions: Tailor questions to the specifics of the project or litigation. For example, inquire about any shared projects, key discussions, or transactions in which they participated.

Data Migration/Access History: Ask whether they have transferred or accessed files from legacy systems (e.g., previous archiving systems or older cloud platforms). This can reveal historical data not immediately visible in current systems.

Data Storage Practices: Inquire where the custodian typically stores their work data (local drives, personal devices, cloud, etc.) and any specific repositories they access. This will inform the scope of data collection.

Documentation and Reporting

Maintain Interview Records: Document the key findings from each interview, including any specific data sources identified and the custodian's data retention practices.

Generate a Custodian Report: Create a detailed report summarizing the custodian's involvement, identified data sources, and the steps taken to preserve and collect that data.

Chain of Custody: Establish and document the chain of custody for all data collected, ensuring every action is traceable and defensible during legal proceedings.

Data Mapping

The practice of data mapping has been vital to eDiscovery for many years. Data mapping tools can provide significant advantages in tracking historical custodian information. By mapping data sources across departments, teams, and applications, legal teams gain a comprehensive view of where data has been stored and managed over time.

This data is often contained in legacy or archive systems. Archive systems can range from no-frills file storage solutions that only provide information about the data from a metadata level to fully indexed platforms that provide immediate content and metadata search.

Other purpose-built archive environments, such as Arctera Alta, Proofpoint, Mimecast, and Cloudficient Expireon, provide storage solutions with value-added benefits such as preservation, search, and export to downstream review.

Collaborate with IT departments to ensure the mapping of all potential ESI sources, including any legacy or archive environments.

Third-Party Systems Integration

As you build your data map, you may find data hosted in third-party applications or environments, or data that may be accessible to your applications but stored in a proprietary format. In this case, you may have to rely on Application Programming Interfaces (APIs) or connectors to populate information in your data map for these sources.

APIs act as bridges, enabling seamless communication and data exchange between an organization's internal systems and external repositories such as cloud storage, SaaS platforms, or vendor-managed databases.

APIs provide a standardized way for systems to interact programmatically, ensuring data from third-party platforms can be accessed, queried, and imported into eDiscovery tools without manual intervention. For instance, APIs can retrieve specific data sets, apply filters, and automate importation into eDiscovery platforms like Relativity or Nuix. This eliminates inefficiencies caused by exporting and reformatting files manually.

Connectors, often built into advanced eDiscovery solutions, offer pre-configured pathways for specific third-party platforms such as Microsoft 365, Google Workspace, or Salesforce. These connectors simplify the identification process by mapping the data structure of third-party systems to the eDiscovery environment. They enable legal teams to access files, emails, and metadata directly, reducing the risk of missing crucial information.

Benefits of Using APIs and Connectors:

Streamlined Data Access: Automatically synchronize third-party data sources with data maps, ensuring consistent updates and reducing the time spent locating relevant data.

Improved Accuracy: Minimize errors in data transfer through automated processes that adhere to predefined rules and compliance standards.

Enhanced Visibility: Gain real-time insights into data residing in external systems, enabling a comprehensive overview of custodians and repositories during identification.

By incorporating APIs and connectors into the identification phase, legal and IT teams can manage third-party data sources effectively, supporting a more robust and efficient eDiscovery process.

Getting Started and Quick Wins

An effective identification process takes some time to implement fully. Establishing solid foundational practices and implementing quick wins can mitigate risks, enhance compliance, and streamline legal workflows. This section provides some guidance and quick wins to help start the process.

Create a Template for Case Context

Use an intake form or checklist to ensure all necessary case details, such as involved parties, key individuals, timelines, and potential data sources, are captured.

Develop an Identification Plan

Draft a clear plan that outlines steps for identifying relevant ESI, including roles, responsibilities, and timelines. Ensure the plan accommodates manual processes and any deployed tools or technologies.

Helpful Advice: Include a validation step to cross-check findings against the initial data map and custodian insights, ensuring completeness.

Implement Custodian Mapping

Implement a custodian mapping solution such as Cloudficient CaseFusion:Identify or interview custodians to map their roles, responsibilities, and data management practices. Doing so ensures a comprehensive understanding of potential data sources.

Helpful Advice: Build reports for high-profile custodian targets from the custodian management solution. Alternatively, a spreadsheet can document custodians, their reporting structures, and the systems they use for data storage.

Create a Custodian Interview Template

Create questionnaires tailored to custodians' roles to streamline the data-gathering process and reduce the risk of oversight. Test the template and process by staging a mock custodian interview with one or two departments to fine-tune the interview checklist.

Launch Data Mapping and Classification

Conduct a focused data mapping exercise to locate critical datasets. Classify these datasets based on their importance to legal, regulatory, and business operations.

Custodians and potentially relevant data sets will vary from case to case. Starting this exercise by mapping data sets to departments or work groups is an easy way to make the identification stage of a future case more efficient.

Helpful Advice: Begin with a single department or business unit to create a scalable model for broader implementation.

Assess Data Management Practices

Examine how data is currently managed within the identified repositories. Look for outdated storage practices, overreliance on personal devices, or lack of consistent data handling protocols.

Helpful Advice: Initiate collaboration with IT to begin reviewing key systems' access permissions and usage logs to identify potential risks or anomalies.

Activate Data Access Logs

Audit logs can be a valuable tool during investigations. They track and keep a record of file metadata, allowing legal teams to identify who created, opened, or edited a file and when the action occurred.

Proactively enable audit logging for systems housing critical data to improve traceability and identify potential compliance gaps. This also sets the stage for access log tracing for future matters.

Establish Reporting Dashboards

Create simple, visual dashboards highlighting key metrics such as storage cost reductions, compliance improvements, or legal hold effectiveness.

Helpful Advice: Use widely available tools like Excel or Tableau to produce these reports quickly and cost-effectively.

Conclusion

This chapter explored the essential tools and techniques that strengthen the eDiscovery identification process, focusing on bridging gaps between legal and IT teams to enhance efficiency and accuracy. Custodian mapping emerges as a cornerstone of this phase, offering a structured approach to linking employees with their roles, data ownership, and potential repositories of electronically stored information (ESI). By documenting these connections through manual efforts and specialized tools like Cloudficient CaseFusion, organizations gain a comprehensive view of their data landscape, ensuring no critical sources are overlooked. These insights also support early case assessment (ECA), enabling legal teams to evaluate the scope and relevance of evidence early in the process.

In addition to custodian mapping, custodian interviews provide an indispensable method for gathering nuanced information about data creation and storage habits. Through tailored preparation and clear communication, interviews uncover essential details about data repositories, compliance practices, and the use of both personal and external systems. This information informs subsequent steps in eDiscovery, ensuring a thorough and defensible identification process.

This chapter also emphasized the importance of data mapping and third-party integration. Data mapping identifies the locations of relevant information across internal and external systems, including legacy and archival platforms, while collaboration with IT departments ensures comprehensive coverage. Advanced tools such as APIs and data connectors streamline the integration of third-party systems like cloud storage and SaaS platforms, reducing manual intervention and maintaining compliance. By combining structured methodologies with cutting-edge technologies, legal and IT teams can achieve greater precision and readiness during the identification stage of eDiscovery.

What's Next

The natural progression in an eDiscovery workflow after identification focuses on **preservation**, ensuring that the identified ESI is securely held to meet legal and regulatory requirements. This involves:

Establishing Legal Hold Protocols: Transitioning from identification to issuing and monitoring legal holds to prevent data spoliation.

Enhancing Data Integrity: Ensuring identified data remains tamper-proof and defensible in court.

Collaboration Continuity: Strengthening the cross-functional relationships established during identification to support ongoing preservation efforts.

The next chapter focuses on preservation planning and sets the stage for an efficient and legally sound transition from identification to the remaining stages of eDiscovery workflows.

Part III: Preservation

Chapter 5: The Duty to Preserve ESI

In Part III, we will focus on the legal duty to preserve evidence when litigation occurs or is anticipated. Failure to meet this duty can lead to sanctions imposed by a court up to and including a default judgment.

Key Themes in This Chapter

- The Importance of Preserving ESI
- Spoliation of Evidence
- Preservation Planning
- The Differences Between Preservation and Collection of ESI
- The Impact of Document Versions on Preservation
- When the Duty to Preserve Ends
- Releasing Litigation Holds

The Importance of Preserving ESI

The duty to preserve evidence in litigation has its roots in the Common Law of England ("common law" is a system of jurisprudence where legal precedent is established through court decisions rather than written laws or statutes). Related duties can also arise from other sources such as contracts, regulations or statutes, a voluntary assumption, or other sources. Essentially, the duty requires parties to preserve all physical and electronic evidence that may be relevant to potential claims when litigation is reasonably likely. What constitutes "reasonably likely"? What "evidence" might be "relevant"? What claims are reasonable to anticipate at the outset versus later?

Analyzing these questions typically spans the content of more than four law school courses on eDiscovery[3] and is beyond the scope of this book. However, we will provide practical tips to execute the duty to preserve and leave the determination of its trigger to you and your counsel.

A word of caution related to this evolving body of law: new data types and communication methods require attorneys to constantly evaluate preservation methods, including preservation letters, ESI protocol templates, discovery request templates, and legal hold notices/memoranda. Courts are becoming increasingly less forgiving of counsel claiming they did not understand the technologies their clients were using when defending against spoliation claims. What exactly is spoliation?

Spoliation: Failure to Preserve

Spoliation is the legal term for failing to preserve evidence once the duty has been triggered. Courts can sanction a party for both negligent and intentional spoliation of evidence. The court has discretion when sanctioning parties, ranging from ordering a party to redo portions of the eDiscovery workflow at their expense to more outcome-determinative sanctions like an adverse inference instruction (instructing the jury it should assume the missing evidence would have been harmful to the party that failed to produce it) or even a default judgment (entering a judgment in the case in favor of the party that requested the missing evidence). In addition, motions to compel brought under Rule 37 of the Federal

---

[3] Brandon co-taught a skills-based eDiscovery course at the Charleston School of Law with Professor Allyson Haynes, including the first version of the course in 2014. The course blends caselaw with practical exercises designed to prepare students for eDiscovery in practice.

Rules of Civil Procedure allow the court to award reasonable attorneys' fees and expenses to the prevailing party. [4] Because of the technical nature of these claims, experts may be hired, and counsel on both sides may bill many hours for preparing and arguing motions.

The number of cases involving the spoliation of ESI is rising as parties' employees use new data types and messaging platforms. Implementing the preservation strategies in this book and ensuring both inside and outside counsel are knowledgeable about the data sources used by the custodians in the case will go a long way toward preventing spoliation.

Questions you should ask include:

- How is data stored, and in what format?
- How long is data typically retained in the application?
- Is data retained after deletion, and, if so, for how long?
- Are copies or backups of the data replicated to other locations?
- Is the data encrypted in such a way that makes extraction difficult?
- Does the application have a native function to export the data in a format suitable for eDiscovery?
- Is any data protected by contractual, legal, or regulatory obligations such that a protective order should be entered?

We suggest corporate counsel record the answers to these questions in a central location to make working with outside counsel easier

---

[4] *See* Fed. R. Civ. P. 37(a) granting the court discretion to award fees and costs. *See also* Fed. R. Civ. P. 37(e) ("Failure to Preserve Electronically Stored Information")

and ensure counsel is informed when negotiating ESI Protocols with opposing counsel or making representations to the court.

Preservation Planning

Planning your preservation strategy typically involves several steps, depending on where data resides, who is considered a custodian of that data, and whether it is in the party's possession, custody, or control. Each of these factors is vitally important because you may not get a second chance to preserve relevant ESI due to automated deletion policies, user behavior, or the routine use of business systems. We will address each of these separately.

Data Location

Data location is a multi-faceted concept. It can refer to the system in which the data is created, the system where it is stored, or the geographic location of the data. All of these can impact your preservation strategy.

The system in which the data is created will generally have processes and limitations on how data can be searched and exported. You must fully understand any limitations, such as non-searchable or non-indexed fields, the system's evaluation of search terms, and whether data is exported to facilitate downstream eDiscovery analysis and review. Also, does the system support preservation in place – that is, does the system have built-in "legal hold" functionality? Some popular collaboration platforms allow administrators to preserve data such that end users and retention/deletion policies are unable to alter the data once the hold has been implemented.

Another consideration is whether a more accessible copy of the data exists. Many business systems have different search syntax or underlying technology and confusing or incomplete legal hold features, making preservation across multiple systems risky. If a copy of the same data exists in an archive, that system will likely have a more extensive eDiscovery toolset, ensuring your preservation strategy is more uniformly executed and that it takes many of the variables of production business systems from the equation.

Geographic location can be an issue due to privacy laws in foreign jurisdictions. Any preservation plan that involves international data must account for relevant privacy laws. It is important to understand, for example, whether data must be processed and reviewed in the country where it was created and stored or if data containing Personally Identifiable Information (PII) must be deidentified before transmitting it across borders. A complete discussion of cross-border eDiscovery is beyond the scope of this book. Still, we encourage you to consider data residency requirements from an information governance and business perspective and their impacts on eDiscovery based on your company's or client's litigation profile. The bottom line is that you should, whenever possible, minimize the data that must be transferred between countries for eDiscovery.

Who (or What) Is a Custodian?

Generally, a custodian of ESI is a natural person who creates, receives, or stores data. For example, if I send or receive an email, chat message, WhatsApp message, text message, or voice message, I am the custodian of all the above. Similarly, if I create a document or file and/or store, share, transmit, or otherwise interact with the file, I am a custodian of that file. This could include photos, drawings, spreadsheets, presentations, notes, memos, many other file types, and records created in structured systems like a CRM or project management system.

What if a team, such as marketing or sales, has a shared location to store ESI, such as a OneDrive folder, Google Drive folder, or a SharePoint site? Here, the concept of a custodian tends to get grayer. Many practitioners consider the team a custodian of all the files, and this is more a function of how data will be organized later in review rather than a precise definition of custodian. When individuals interact with those files, they, in fact, could be considered custodians of those files. They have knowledge of and may have contributed to the content. That information will be important later in review, deposition prep, and maybe even trial prep.

When developing your preservation plan, it is important to consider how you will analyze the files later in review and how you will ensure important metadata is made available to reviewers and the trial team. Will you assign teams as custodians for shared resources, individuals at the file level, or both? Modern custodian identification platforms like Cloudficient's CaseFusion can provide insight into who interacted with files in shared repositories so custodian ownership can be determined with greater precision.

When notifying individual custodians of their duty to preserve ESI, a technical custodian should also be notified to preserve ESI in shared repositories. Typically, this will be the application or infrastructure administrator in IT.

Possession, Custody, or Control

Another issue that affects preservation is the legal concept of possession, custody, or control. The duty to preserve evidence extends to evidence that is in the possession, custody, or control of the producing party. This concept is fairly black and white when it comes to legacy on-premises systems, but it can be less clear with cloud data sources, third-party data, and even data stored on employees' personal devices. Jurisdictions may differ in their interpretation of these concepts, so it is important to understand the precedent in a particular jurisdiction when advising clients on what ESI may be in their possession, custody, or control. Issues like control may even stem from how an agency relationship is interpreted in that jurisdiction. Courts may also look to contracts and company policies, such as acceptable use policies and Bring Your Own Device (BYOD) policies to understand the extent of control exerted on data stored on third-party devices or systems.

Preservation vs. Collection

The actions of preservation and collection of ESI are distinct and warrant separate discussion, but the practice of "collecting to preserve" is something we will discuss and contrast with "preserving in place."

When does it make sense to collect the ESI at the point of preservation? If the target system is volatile (e.g. an ephemeral messaging app like Signal that only stores messages for a limited time), then the only copy may be on a personal mobile device, which is subject to being damaged or erased. Or, if the system does not allow administrators to guarantee that data is immutable, it should be collected to ensure the data is preserved and does not get altered by users or routine operation of the system. Collection may simply mean making a copy of the data and storing it on immutable storage.

Preservation in place should be reserved for data sources or data locations that offer legal hold features and preserve data in an immutable fashion. Productivity and collaboration suites like Microsoft M365, Google Workspace, and Slack offer native legal hold functionality. It is important to understand the nuances of these systems because the legal hold features differ across all of them. Because the bulk of eDiscovery data will likely come from a system like this, it is an attractive proposition to preserve the data in place until needed for processing and review. We suggest spending some time reviewing documentation for each system's legal hold features, especially where those features differ among data types or communication channels.

A third option, archiving, which we have mentioned a few times already, involves moving the data immediately as it is created to a secure archive where eDiscovery tasks can be more easily and consistently performed. This process for email is called journaling, but the same concept can be applied to file system data in OneDrive, SharePoint data, chat data in Teams and Slack, and even mobile device communications. If a company has a high volume of eDiscovery and other matters that require preservation and collection of ESI, the efficiency gains and overall risk reduction of using an archive more than justifies the cost. ESI can be safely and securely preserved in place in the archive while scope for review is further refined or counsel negotiates a phased approach to eDiscovery.

Which Version Should You Preserve?

Side effects of modern collaboration technologies are shared documents and their version history. These platforms are great when you want to roll back document changes or look back to see what changes were made at a specific point in time, or even maintain versions for updates to a policy document, but this practice can create challenges in eDiscovery.

If you send an email including a hyperlink to a document in a shared cloud repository, and that email must be preserved one year later for discovery, which version of the document should be preserved (if any)? Is it the current version, including any changes that have occurred over the last year, as well as the removal of data that was present when it was first linked in the email, or the version at the time the email was sent? Or neither, because a hyperlink is not an attachment? This issue, at the time of writing, is largely unsettled and depends on the facts of the individual case. Many challenges currently exist in M365 and Google Workspace regarding preservation of the "contemporaneous version" of a shared document.

The answer to which version should be preserved may also be limited by the capabilities of systems in use by the parties. It is critical, though, for counsel on both sides to understand what is possible given the systems in use by a party, as well as the capabilities of third-party tools. As companies adopt modern eDiscovery platforms such as CaseFusion (mentioned above), it will become much easier to preserve contemporaneous versions as well as determine what activity was performed on which documents and when – without manually inspecting version history one document at a time. Modern archives can also assist with fetching the contemporaneous version as an email or chat message so it is preserved along with the communication, making the preserved data more like traditional attachments. It's good to have options, right?

When Does the Duty to Preserve End?

The logical next question after what to preserve and how to preserve it is how long must it be preserved? The answer to that question depends on several procedural factors related to the litigation or triggering event.

The general rule is you must preserve potentially relevant ESI until the litigation has concluded or litigation is no longer reasonably likely. There are several ways the litigation may end: settlement, dismissal with prejudice, or entering a judgment. When plaintiffs in multiple jurisdictions could bring claims in the future, the disposition of a case in one jurisdiction may not absolve the party of its duty to preserve ESI. A best practice is to have counsel thoroughly analyze other potential claims related to those in the underlying litigation and the potential for appeals before releasing litigation holds and resuming the automatic deletion of ESI per company retention policies.

Additionally, litigants are sometimes tempted to release holds or resume automatic deletion of data in production systems once initial collection is complete. We have seen enough cases where the scope changes, the collected data was corrupt, or some other technical issue required recollection, that we recommend preserving data in the underlying data repositories as long as possible – ideally until the overall duty to preserve ends. You may end up preserving more data than you ultimately collect (or agree to produce) but having access to the data years later when you realize you have to perform additional collections could save you from a burdensome and expensive spoliation dispute.

Conclusion

The duty to preserve electronically stored information (ESI) is critical to legal and regulatory compliance. As explored in this chapter, the duty to preserve is a legal obligation originating in the common law, but it is impacted by several factors and a proactive measure to mitigate risks of spoliation and associated sanctions and penalties.

Key elements such as understanding the triggers for the duty to preserve, effectively managing preservation plans, and navigating the nuanced differences between preservation and collection form the foundation of defensible practices. These strategies are further complicated by the dynamic nature of technology, which demands ongoing adaptation to new communication tools, data types, and storage methods. A thorough understanding of an organization's technology landscape and IG policies ensures practitioners can navigate these challenges while maintaining compliance.

Preservation efforts are most effective when approached collaboratively, involving legal, IT, and business teams to align goals and responsibilities. Organizations can establish robust frameworks that support legal defensibility and operational efficiency by integrating thoughtful planning, clear communication, and the right technological tools. This preparation protects against the legal repercussions of spoliation and reinforces trust in the organization's governance and compliance practices.

Ultimately, the principles and practices outlined in this chapter empower organizations to uphold their legal obligations while fostering a culture of accountability and precision in handling ESI.

What's Next

The next chapter will review actionable steps organizations can take to implement effective preservation strategies. Building on the foundational understanding of the duty to preserve ESI, the next chapter provides practical steps focusing on:

- **Implementing Legal Holds**: Guidance on drafting, distributing, and managing legal hold notices to ensure compliance with preservation obligations.
- **Tools and Technology**: Exploration of advanced eDiscovery tools and automated processes that streamline preservation workflows.
- **Data Integrity and Best Practices**: Insights into forensic imaging, encryption, and other techniques that safeguard data integrity during preservation.
- **Managing Modern Data Sources**: Strategies to address the challenges of preserving data from cloud environments, hybrid infrastructures, mobile devices, and emerging communication platforms.
- **Documentation and Audit Trails**: Techniques that emphasize the importance of maintaining defensible records to mitigate risks and demonstrate compliance when practices are scrutinized.

Chapter 6 focuses on practical procedures and leveraging of modern tools, equipping readers with the knowledge to address preservation challenges and establish robust, defensible processes proactively.

Chapter 6: Practical Approaches to Preservation

Key Themes in This Chapter

- Drafting and managing legal holds
- Preserving ESI in place
- Collecting ESI for preservation
- Preservation of portable media
- Where and how to store preserved ESI

Drafting and Managing Legal Holds

What is a Legal Hold?

A legal hold is simply a written instruction or set of instructions, typically drafted and issued by lawyers to custodians, that informs custodians and other interested parties about their role in a party's (usually the company's) duty to preserve ESI. Effective legal holds involve several steps which we define in this chapter. Legal holds are issued on both sides of litigation. If a party is an individual, they may receive a preservation letter from their counsel or opposing counsel, but in the corporate setting, legal holds should be issued to all identified custodians.

Requirements for legal holds, including how they are issued, what they should include, and how they should be managed, are determined by case law. In the landmark *Zubulake*[5] opinions, Judge

---

[5] See Zubulake v. UBS Warburg, LLC, 229 F.R.D. 422 (S.D.N.Y. 2004) ("Zubulake V") for discussion of legal hold requirements and expectations of counsel.

Shira Scheindlin laid out probably the most comprehensive set of instructions for what is expected of counsel when issuing and managing legal holds. The federal rules, specifically Rule 26, also provide guidance of what is expected of parties in discovery but look to cases like *Zubulake* and subsequent cases to interpret the rules and provide practical instructions (or cautionary tales).

Imagine for a moment that you have spent hours crafting the perfect legal hold memo to send to all the custodians you have identified in your matter. You have painstakingly drafted each word to ensure maximum understanding and compliance, and you spent extra time explaining all the data sources that could contain relevant ESI. You send it as an attachment to an email, and you even get a few replies from custodians assuring you that they have received it. Then, when conducting custodian interviews a few weeks later, a custodian tells you that they just had their computer wiped and reimaged by IT. This custodian never actually read the legal hold memo and assumed that the interview would explain everything.

This situation may not lead to spoliation sanctions, but it could. What steps were missing from this process? Counsel must manage the legal hold, track compliance, and take affirmative steps to ensure compliance. This is at the heart of Judge Scheindlin's instructions in *Zubulake*. Counsel cannot simply send a legal hold memo and then never revisit the process until data is being collected for processing and review.

Legal Hold Requirements

Drafting Tips

The most important goal of a legal hold communication is that the custodian understands the requirement to preserve ESI and what to preserve. A popular AI prompt these days is, "Explain it like I'm five." We think this is a great guideline for legal hold communications, with a slight modification: "Explain it like I'm five and I work at this company." The legal hold should be drafted with this corporate vernacular in mind. It should feel as much like an internal corporate memo as possible.

You also must issue a legal hold when litigation commences or is reasonably anticipated. In other words, the legal hold should be issued as soon as possible after the duty to preserve is triggered. Therefore, if you are working with a defendant, the only information you may have to go on regarding the plaintiff's claims is the complaint. You should synthesize those claims and draft the legal hold to encompass all potentially relevant ESI related to those claims. However, you should not simply copy and paste the claims into the legal hold. Remember the most important goal? Custodians must be able to easily understand their obligations. Translate the claims into categories of information familiar to custodians.

Legal holds can be communicated to custodians using different methods depending on the technology preferences or tools used by the company. Generally, custodians initially receive an email, and if the company does not have a legal hold software tool, that email may just contain an attached document explaining the legal hold in detail. Several legal hold notification solutions exist that automate the sending of emails and may even allow custodians to click a link in the email that displays the legal hold text on a webpage.

However you choose to deliver the legal hold to custodians, it must be in writing, and we recommend you open that communication explaining what a legal hold is and why it is important. Do not assume a custodian knows anything about this process, and you should assume receiving a legal hold email may cause some distress or anxiety. Explain they are not under investigation and let them know the legal department is available to walk them through the hold and answer any questions they have. Encourage them to ask questions or for clarification immediately – do NOT wait for interviews or for future communication.

Also, be specific. We intentionally used the word "instructions" above. Here are a few examples of bad outcomes you can preempt with great instructions:

1. *Mobile device data automatically deleted:* Instruct custodians to change their device settings to disable any automatic deletion (especially with respect to text messages and ephemeral communication apps like Telegram or Signal).
2. *Data not preserved in departmental apps:* Explain to custodians that if their team uses applications specific to their department, they need to let the legal department know. This data could be relevant to the matter and should be preserved until they consult with the legal team. Many custodians assume IT takes care of preserving data for them. Let them know these unique apps may require special handling for preservation and collection. The sooner you can begin investigating that, the better off you will be.
3. *A device is damaged, or data is wiped:* Let custodians know they should let IT know they are on legal hold before any work is done on their devices. If they use a personal device for business communications or to create data for work, they should contact the legal department before any service is performed on that device (or if it is damaged). A better practice is to instruct custodians to notify the legal department immediately if they use their mobile device for business so arrangements can be made to collect relevant

data as soon as possible. If one of these devices is destroyed with no attempt made to collect that data for preservation, and the data on the device is not backed up, destruction of the device will not be a defense to spoliation.

4. *Custodians reply to the legal hold email with dozens of emails and documents:* Be sure to specify whether you want custodians to send relevant ESI directly to the legal department. We typically do not recommend doing this without very specific instructions. Custodians may initially send data and think their obligation is complete. Or, because they do not have forensic or legal training, they may provide an incomplete collection. If you believe certain key custodians possess documents that will help with early case strategy, send specific instructions to those custodians to retrieve those files (and still plan to collect them along with other ESI).

After defining a legal hold, explaining the custodian's role, and giving specific instructions on what to preserve and how to preserve it, you may also want to note any next steps. Will you conduct custodian interviews or send out surveys to custodians to collect information related to ESI sources, additional custodians, or case facts? Let them know what to expect and when to expect it.

Finally, with an increasing public focus on privacy and data security, custodians may be apprehensive about their data being collected, especially if personal devices are involved. Explain any safeguards you are putting in place to maintain the confidentiality of their personal data (to the extent it may be collected) or the steps you have implemented to ensure only business data is collected. This could be as simple as working with the custodian during the collection process or having a third-party examiner review the device data, so other employees cannot inadvertently view personal data of any custodian.

Like any document related to the litigation sent by counsel, include the words "attorney-client privilege" and "work product" to ensure you can easily filter documents and message threads containing them during document review.

Managing the Legal Hold

Counsel is also responsible for ensuring custodians understand the legal hold and that they have or will comply. Effective management and documentation includes the following elements:

1. *Recording acknowledgement:*
   A record should be kept of each custodian affirmatively acknowledging they have received the legal hold, they understand it, and they will comply. This acknowledgment can be done via a physical signature, but most companies use an electronic confirmation. Legal hold software platforms, like Cloudficient CaseFusion, provide a web portal for custodians to review the legal hold and electronically acknowledge it. That action is recorded and maintained as part of the audit trail for the legal hold process. Custodians can then review the legal hold at any time in the future if they need a refresher.

   CaseFusion also provides the ability to create multiple points of acknowledgment in the web portal, akin to requiring someone to initial important terms of a contract in addition to signing. This can be useful to track compliance with and completion of specific instructions or tasks in the legal hold. Each acknowledgment should be tracked with a separate date and time stamp.

2. *Escalating if no response:*
   A best practice is to set a threshold number of days (or even hours) for custodians to acknowledge the legal hold. Set the expectation clearly in the legal hold communication and convey the consequences if they do not respond (ex. escalation to their manager, a division leader, the legal team, etc.). This can also be automated using legal hold software, but if you must manage it manually, ensure you can review the acknowledgments received so you can quickly identify who has not yet responded. An employee could be on vacation, traveling or simply have been busy. There are dozens of reasons why someone may not respond, but it is imperative to determine t and track the outstanding responses to completion. Leveraging employees' manager(s) can help scale your efforts, but you must still manage the process to ensure the managers are doing their part.

3. *Re-issuing to new employees:*
   Custodians are often identified based on their team or role at the company. What happens when you hire new employees into the same role or team? They should be added to the legal hold as soon as possible because they may be creating new data relevant to the matter, and the duty to preserve is an *ongoing duty*. If you have been documenting each step taken for other custodians, guiding a new employee through the same process should be straightforward.

Issuing periodic reminders: All custodians should receive periodic written reminders of the legal hold. These communications can be a single reminder at a set interval (for example, quarterly) for every legal hold and every custodian, or a legal hold reminder digest email (also quarterly) informing custodians that holds are still active and their duty to preserve data is ongoing. If you are using legal hold software, this process can be easily created and automated, even providing a link to the custodian web portal. Alternatively, could create a database or spreadsheet to list each unique custodian along with the legal holds they are a part of, track the status of each legal hold, and generate reminder emails either through scripting or manual effort.

4. Each of these management tasks can be burdensome on their own. Managing all these tasks for dozens, hundreds, or even thousands of legal holds would be untenable for most teams. This is why many large companies use purpose-built legal hold software. If that software is fully integrated with modules for identification and collection, it provides a complete foundational eDiscovery platform to automate and audit these workflows in a defensible manner.

Releasing Legal Holds

Releasing a legal hold simply involves notifying custodians the matter is resolved, and the company no longer has a duty to preserve ESI *related to that matter*. It is very important to state very plainly the custodian may be subject to other active legal holds. Providing a link to the custodian portal in that communication is even better, or alternatively, listing the other legal holds in the release email.

When sending the release to custodians, you should also inform IT admins, who may have suspended automatic deletion procedures in production systems. They may elect to resume automatic deletion if they are able to do so without affecting other legal holds. It is also important to let IT admins know which custodians are still on other active legal holds.

Are Legal Holds Discoverable?

You may be wondering if all these legal hold notices, emails, documentation, and other artifacts are discoverable. The short answer is no, not usually. If, however, the legal hold procedure itself is called into question, these materials could be discoverable by opposing counsel, or at a minimum, reviewed by the court.

Generally, when a dispute arises about the procedure of preservation (or other discovery responses), and the parties cannot work it out on their own within the framework of the ESI protocol or scheduling order, the receiving party should file a motion under Rule 30(b)(6)[6] requiring the producing party to produce a witness with knowledge of the company's systems and processes, as well as the specific steps taken in discovery.

If you are the party required to produce the 30(b)(6) witness, it pays to make sure that witness is thoroughly prepared. This person can be a dedicated eDiscovery professional, an employee from IT, or even a consultant. Select the person who would have the most knowledge about the aspect of discovery at issue.

---

6 Fed. R. Civ. P. 30(b)(6).

Preserving ESI in Place

In eDiscovery, the phrase "preserve in place" simply means ESI is preserved in the original system where it was created or is currently being stored. The alternative, "collect to preserve," means copying the data in a forensically sound manner from the target system to a dedicated preservation store, like Cloudficient Expireon. We will explore the much more complex question of when to preserve in place versus collecting to preserve ESI.

When to Preserve in Place

You should only preserve ESI in place when you can be assured end users cannot alter the data, including modifying the metadata or content of existing documents or files. If that sounds impossible, it generally is for any production system being accessed by employees. The only exception is when that system has built in legal hold features that allow copies to be stored alongside the original files. Microsoft Purview, for example, can be used to preserve users' content in place, but it is done at a custodian level, so if a custodian received an email from a co-worker that included a link to a document stored in the co-worker's SharePoint site or OneDrive account, that file would not be on legal hold. It is critically important to understand the limitations of these systems even if they have built-in preservation features. This is also a valid reason to ensure your custodian mapping and identification processes are as thorough as possible. Identifying that coworker as a potential custodian could have allowed sooner preservation of their ESI (as opposed to discovering the email with the hyperlink months into document review).

Other Considerations for Preservation in Place

Some systems may provide a way to suspend automatic purging or deletion, but this is not the same as creating an immutable copy that cannot be modified by end users. For these systems, suspending automatic deletion would be a first step, but to defensibly preserve the ESI, you must ensure it is stored in a manner that does not allow end users to modify content or metadata. That may require collecting or moving the ESI to a preservation store.

Another important consideration for a preserve-in-place strategy is the cost of preserving the data for what could be a very long time. Will the application or storage vendor bill more for keeping copies of this data longer? Will accounts for employees who later leave the company be billed if they need to be preserved after deactivation of the account?

Take time to document the preservation features of frequently targeted systems, and review your vendor contracts or license terms to understand the implications of storing the data on legal hold for long periods of time. In some instances, it may be more cost-effective to collect the ESI and store it safely in a dedicated preservation store.

When to Collect for Preservation

Most departmental and mobile applications do not have built-in preservation capabilities, so you need to collect ESI from these systems to preserve it. Since these systems are likely actively being used by employees, time is of the essence when using a collect-to-preserve strategy.

We will cover collection in depth in the following two chapters. From a preservation perspective, it is critical to understand when to collect vs. preserving in place. If you cannot validate the preservation features in your target systems are sufficient (i.e., they retain the data in an immutable fashion and retain each version of that data if it is actively being used), then you should collect to preserve.

The Ongoing Duty to Preserve

One caveat of a collect-to-preserve strategy is each party has an ongoing duty to preserve relevant ESI, meaning any newly created data relevant to the matter must also be preserved. Some matters deal squarely with a set date range in the past, so other than attorney work product related to the matter, no new data is likely being created. In those instances, the discovery requests will likely be restricted to the date range in question, so you should ensure the scheduling order or ESI protocol stipulates the date range for which custodial ESI will be preserved.

If the events or actions at issue in the litigation are ongoing, the discovery requests may ask for relevant ESI from a particular date in the past *"to the present."* In that scenario, you should work out a schedule of regular collections that can be memorialized in the scheduling order or ESI protocol. Taking this proactive step protects you if data is created and then deleted between collections.

Journaling or other technologies that write a second copy of data as it is created ensure users cannot inadvertently delete data before it can be collected. The journaled or copied data is not accessible by end users, so collections can be performed at regular intervals without concern about the data being modified or deleted. Many solutions allow you to select which mailboxes or accounts to journal. This method can be very effective when preservation in place is not preferred or ongoing collection would be burdensome.

What About Portable Media?

It is likely some employees are still using portable media, at least to some degree (including USB/Thunderbolt drives and SD Cards) to store ESI. We want to emphasize that you should NOT simply hold these storage devices somewhere until you are ready to process the ESI for review. As soon as possible, safely test the media to ensure it can be accessed and is not damaged, especially if you or the custodian believe it contains relevant ESI. Also, because of the volatile nature of portable media, it is recommended you transfer the ESI in a forensically sound manner to a preservation store. Discovering later that the media is defective is not a defense against spoliation, especially if the opposing party can prove the media contained relevant documents otherwise unavailable.

Where and How to Store Preserved ESI

At various stages of the eDiscovery workflow, it is likely that collected ESI will need to be stored. As a best practice, you should store a pristine copy of all data collected and preserved for the duration of the legal hold period. In the case something goes wrong later like the data corrupted in transit or damaged during a downstream process, this action ensures you have another copy that can be used in its place.

A dedicated preservation store provides an additional layer of protection by limiting access and avoiding storage systems used by other production applications. Cloudficient's Expireon, for example, provides immutable storage for ESI along with eDiscovery features not found on simple cloud storage. Expireon is also fully integrated with CaseFusion so data can be added to cases and preserved from that application as part of a full identification and preservation workflow.

At a minimum, ensure your preservation store is secured via access controls to a limited group of individuals and meets all of your organization's security policies for storing sensitive data.

You should also consider where the data will go for processing and review. Choosing a preservation store that provides modern cloud-to-cloud data transfer capabilities can be a huge time saver, avoiding days of copying, encrypting or compressing data, to only then perform the opposite of those steps at the destination.

Getting Started and Quick Wins

Preservation is potentially the most critical step in an eDiscovery workflow. If ESI is not adequately preserved, it cannot be collected, processed, reviewed, or produced. In other words, you can't crack the eggs to make the omelet if the eggs are spoil(iat)ed. Here are some practical things you do immediately to enhance your preservation processes.

Draft a Legal Hold Template

Using the guidelines above, draft a legal hold template you can quickly edit as the duty to preserve is triggered. As we have discussed, time is of the essence, so having a general framework approved by inside and outside counsel speeds up the overall process. If you already use a legal hold template, review it against the guidelines above to ensure it addresses all of them.

Create a Tutorial for Employees

If you are issuing legal holds often, it is a worthwhile investment to create a standard instructional document or video to send or link in the original legal hold notification. Include the basics of what a legal hold is, what custodians should expect, why it is so important for the company to preserve ESI in litigation, and some strategies for ensuring compliance. Think about the compliance and security awareness training videos you have likely had to watch at some point in your career; create something similar for legal holds. You may even be able to distribute or host it on the same platform as your compliance or security training.

Implement a Legal Hold Software System

If you do not have one, investigate implementing a legal hold software system. Cloudficient CaseFusion is a great platform that meets all the requirements listed in this chapter and more. There are several other platforms as well – pick a couple of them, then schedule meetings with the vendors to get a demo. Armed with the knowledge from this chapter, you will be able to ask the right questions to ensure the platform you select meets those requirements.

Discuss Preservation Capabilities for Primary Systems with IT

Set up time with your IT admins to discuss in-place preservation features in your primary systems like email, file sharing, and collaboration platforms. Document these capabilities and even perform preservation steps in the platforms, preferably in a test tenant or with test accounts. If you test with production accounts, make sure none of the accounts are on active legal holds. The more you understand the capabilities of these platforms, the better equipped you will be to build a preservation plan that ensures minimized risk of spoliation. Documenting these features as part of your data map streamlines future matters and helps counsel prepare for early pre-trial events like the Rule 26(f) conference and preparation of the ESI protocol and/or scheduling order.

Conclusion

Preservation in eDiscovery can be challenging. As we have explored throughout this chapter, successful preservation requires a carefully orchestrated combination of clear communication, robust processes, and appropriate technological solutions. From drafting comprehensive legal holds to making strategic decisions about preservation methods, legal teams must approach each step with both diligence and pragmatism.

The choice between preserving ESI in place versus collecting for preservation highlights the complex balancing act legal teams must perform. Understanding the limitations of preservation features in target systems, along with considerations like storage costs and the ongoing duty to preserve, should inform preservation strategy decisions. Additionally, proper handling of portable media and preserving ESI on secure, dedicated preservation stores are essential components of a defensible framework.

Organizations that implement the practices outlined in this chapter will be well-positioned to meet their preservation obligations while minimizing both risk and cost. However, it is important to remember preservation is not a one-size-fits-all proposition – each matter requires careful consideration of its unique circumstances, including the nature of relevant ESI, the capabilities of source systems, and the specific requirements of the case. By taking a thoughtful, systematic approach to preservation and leveraging appropriate tools and technologies, legal teams can create efficient, defensible processes that serve as the foundation for successful eDiscovery operations.

What's Next

In Part 4, we move on to collecting ESI in eDiscovery. We take you through the planning, execution, and defensibility of collections for many different data types, noting potential issues and preparing you for them.

We will cover:

Creating and tailoring a collection plan: Building a collection plan for each matter based on the requirements and data types involved.

Common challenges in collection: Identifying challenges in collection and how to prepare for and mitigate them.

Collection techniques and methods: From targeted collections to remote collections.

Advanced tools for collection: Automation and validation techniques to improve efficiency and defensibility.

Part IV: Collection

Chapter 7: Introduction to Collection in eDiscovery

This chapter explores the pivotal role of the collection phase in eDiscovery. Collection involves gathering ESI that has been identified and preserved, focusing on ensuring accuracy, efficiency, and defensibility to prepare the ESI for processing and review. It highlights the strategic planning required for effective data collection, the importance of scoping and aligning efforts with legal and compliance standards, and the challenges posed by diverse data sources. By emphasizing collaboration across legal, IT, and business teams, this chapter provides a foundation for navigating the technical and procedural complexities of the collection phase.

Key Themes in This Chapter

- Understanding the Collection Phase of eDiscovery
- Strategic Planning and
  Accurate Scoping
- Ensuring Accuracy, Efficiency, and Defensibility
- Navigating Data Sources and Collection Methods
- Legal and Compliance Considerations

Overview of Collection

The collection phase of eDiscovery is a critical juncture where preserved ESI is gathered for further analysis and review. Unlike preservation, which ensures data is safeguarded, collection involves extracting specific datasets deemed potentially relevant.

Information governance defines effective data management. Identification and preservation define the potential collection data estate. Now, collection focuses on narrowing down, or culling, the data set to only what is required for the matter. As a reminder, a large percentage of eDiscovery costs are in downstream review, so anything that can be done to limit the amount of defensibly collected data will reap benefits in later stages of the workflow.

Errors or omissions at the collection stage can lead to missed deadlines, sanctions, or compromised case outcomes. To ensure a successful collection effort, target the following key objectives::

- **Accuracy**: Collect only what is necessary to reduce downstream review and storage costs.
- **Defensibility**: Maintain strict protocols and documentation to collected data can withstand judicial or regulatory scrutiny.
- **Efficiency**: Streamline the process to meet tight deadlines without compromising compliance or thoroughness.

Strategic Planning

Proper data collection has many components. The first step is effective strategic planning, which involves collaboration between legal, IT, compliance, and business teams.

This planning includes how the collection process will be handled from a project perspective, which requires understanding data sources and their effects on collection.

Defining Objectives and Scope

Once the collection team is assembled, they will analyze the case to determine the effort required to collect the relevant and responsive data. This is where the previous steps of the eDiscovery workflow start to pay dividends.

Many factors must be considered when properly determining the objectives and scope of the collection, which forms the basis of the case strategy.

This team determines the collection method. It must clearly outline what constitutes "relevant" or "responsive" data in the matter's context. The specific methods or scope of collection may be based on an ESI protocol or scheduling order agreed upon by both parties to the matter following a Rule 26(f) conference.[7] Based on the case strategy or negotiated protocols, the team will perform this work with direct input from internal and external legal counsel.

The team will then review the data estate to determine what data to collect.

Custodians and their data sources are reviewed using custodian and data mapping efforts from earlier workflow steps to identify relevant data.

The team then confirms legal hold and preservation efforts are aligned with legal hold and compliance requirements for the entirety of the case.

---

[7] See Fed. R. Civ. P. 26(f)(2): "The attorneys of record and all unrepresented parties that have appeared in the case are jointly responsible for arranging the conference, for attempting in good faith to agree on the proposed discovery plan, and for submitting to the court within 14 days after the conference a written report outlining the plan. The court may order the parties or attorneys to attend the conference in person." Also note some Federal district courts and/or judges have local rules governing discovery plans, conferences, and even ESI protocols that should be reviewed prior to meeting with the opposing party or parties.

Understanding Collection from Data Sources

Collecting data varies from source to source, and many factors can affect the data collected based on available tools and techniques. Each data source is analyzed to determine what types of data (email, chat, files) are hosted by each platform and what tools are available to retrieve data from platform. Some data sources have search and export capabilities, some may provide API access, while others may be closed ecosystems that requires assistance from the vendor.

Custodian-Based Collection or Content Collection

There are typically two types of data collection: custodian–based collection and content collection. Custodian-based collections usually involve a workflow that collects all data for chosen custodians based on a date range. The internal legal team may want to collect data based only on metadata (custodian and date ranges only) and then utilize downstream eDiscovery tools to perform keyword searches during the processing and review phases.

Other protocols may not be defined by custodian. In some instances, the collection may center around keywords or phrases, regardless of where the data resides or who owns it. This is known as a custodian collection.

While custodian-based collections cast a wide net, content collections can drastically reduce the data sent to review.

Search in place or collect and search.

If keyword searches are required or desired, it is important to determine a plan for proper culling via keywords. For platforms with native search and export tools, this process may be straightforward. There are some things to consider when relying on native tools for these efforts.

Some platforms do not have a robust indexing engine, leading to inconsistencies in results when performing keyword searches. Platforms with indexing engines that perform only partial indexing, potentially stop at a specific page limit or file size. For instance, if the platform only indexes the first 2MB of a file, keywords on high-number pages may be missed due to index limitations.

For this reason, some organizations may choose to collect data on a platform that allows for a more robust index and search process. These tools typically can collect data from multiple data sources, consolidating it into one platform for a unified and consistent search experience. These tools utilize an indexing platform that provides full content indexing and handles multiple data formats.

Imagine a scenario where keyword search terms were mutually agreed upon by both parties, but because of differences in indexing and search syntax across multiple systems, the results are inconsistent. This could lead to opposing counsel questioning the integrity of the entire production and lead to expensive and time-consuming motions, especially if the search protocol has been entered as an order by the court.

Hyperlinked Files

Due to the rise in collaboration tools, hyperlinked files (also known as modern attachments, hyperlinked attachments, or internet attachments) introduce challenges to the collection process. A hyperlinked file is often used in collaboration applications (chat, email) to send a link to a file rather than attaching the file to each email or conversation. This allows the sender to provide a link to a collaborative document rather than sending multiple versions back and forth.

Rulings on whether hyperlinked files should be collected have varied recently, with no clear understanding of when or how to collect them. Often, there are technical limitations that make collecting them very challenging and/or time-consuming. Most solutions that provide reactive data collection will collect the linked file as it appears *at the time of collection*. Most legal teams, however, will want to understand what the file looked like when it was attached or linked in the email or the conversation. This version of the file is referred to as the "contemporaneous" version. At this time, only Cloudficient Hyperlize and Cloudficient Expireon can capture the contemporaneous version of these files for Microsoft and Slack applications.

File Revisions

Due to the nature of asynchronous collaboration, file versioning and revisions can complicate the collection process. If multiple people collaborate on a single, shared file, the file may have many versions besides the contemporaneous version. How does one determine which version of the file to include in the collection? Is it the contemporaneous version or the version of the file as it appeared when the custodian first saw it? Is it a version edited on a significant date?

Collecting specific file versions or revisions can be extremely difficult. Most tools only collect the contemporaneous or current version of the file. Collecting a particular version of a file often requires third-party forensic collection tools or engaging an external legal services provider. This is usually a manual process involving a combination of file version information, audit log information with file access and usage information, and file usage information from metadata.

Archive Systems and Legacy Data Sources

Not all data may be live or "active." Some relevant data may reside in archive systems or legacy data sources not currently used by the business. Accessing this type of data during the collection phase of eDiscovery can present significant challenges due to the technological, operational, and cost-related barriers associated with these systems.

Archived data is often stored in formats or systems not designed for quick retrieval. These systems—typically backup tapes, cold storage, or aging email archives—are optimized for long-term retention rather than day-to-day access. Extracting data may require specialized tools or processes, such as restoring data from physical media like tapes, which can be labor-intensive and require costly obsolete technology.

Many archive systems rely on outdated software or hardware that may no longer be supported or compatible with modern IT infrastructure. For example, a legacy email archive might require proprietary software to restore and search the data, but the necessary tools may no longer be available, functional, or supported by the original vendor. Adding additional systems or using "old machinery" solely for eDiscovery purposes is inefficient and cost prohibitive.

Collecting legacy data from these platforms often involves converting it into modern formats, which may result in loss of metadata or changes to the original file structure. If a proper chain of custody is not maintained, these issues can compromise defensibility in court proceedings. Understanding how conversion or extraction of legacy data might affect metadata or even the content of that data is critical.

The Federal Rules of Civil Procedure provide a framework to assess collection of ESI from legacy systems or those deemed inaccessible due to the high burden or cost of retrieving the data. This framework balances the cost of data collection with the amount disputed in the matter and considers whether the information can be retrieved from a more accessible source, if available. Effective custodian and data mapping provides a head start in formulating claims that requested ESI should not be collected due to disproportionate cost or burden.[8]

Ephemeral data

Ephemeral data refers to data that exists for only a short period of time and is designed to disappear automatically after a specific time or event. Platforms like Snapchat, Signal, and similar tools provide configuration options to auto-delete data.

There are many challenges around ephemeral data. Due to its short-lived nature, it is inherently temporary. Unless proactive measures are in place to capture and preserve it, it may be deleted before it can be collected. This creates a risk of spoliation, especially if the duty to preserve has already been triggered.

---

[8] *See* Fed. R. Civ. P. 26(b)(2)(B), 26(b)(2)(C). It is important to note that discovery that can "be obtained from another source" as described in Rule 26(b)(2)(C)(2) does not necessarily mean collecting the same document. Rather, it refers to the content or subject matter. Or put another way, can the question that is to be answered by the produced content be answered with content from another source?

Ephemeral data often exists outside of traditional organizational management. Employees using personal devices or non-approved third-party applications may generate data the organization cannot directly access or preserve without cooperation.

Other risks include data privacy, encryption, lack of metadata, and potential compliance issues for organizations governed by strict regulations such as FINRA or SEC.

Mobile Data

Employees who use mobile devices for work (whether company-issues or personal) often have information stored on smartphones or tablets, including relevant or responsive data such as call logs, text messages, chat app data, location history, emails, photos, and application data.

Some of the same challenges exist with mobile data as with ephemeral data, specifically with encryption and security, application data, and volatile data (recent location cache, temporary files, etc.). Like ephemeral data applications, mobile applications can also be configured to automatically delete data, and custodians may have legitimate reasons for enabling this due to space constraints on their device(s). However, if these applications are being used for business communications, the collection plan must include a protocol for regularly retrieving this data to avoid spoliation.

Not all devices are equal. Phones, tablets, and other devices may have different operating systems (e.g., iOS, Android) and software versions. This makes data collection complex and requires multiple platform tools or methods.

Tailoring the Collection Plan

After analyzing the data sources and collection methods from those data sources, you can start planning the collection. Based on the information gathered from the steps above, you can assess whether the team can complete the collection internally or will need to rely on external resources to perform collection tasks for you.

Each case may have unique requirements based on the industry, jurisdiction, or regulatory environment. For example, GDPR or HIPAA regulations may necessitate specific handling protocols.

Legal and Compliance Implications

Chapters 5 and 6 focus on preservation of ESI, which directly impacts data collection. Data collection is simply a continuation of the duty to preserve ESI and is an intermediate step that facilitates processing and review. Collection can also be used as a preservation step, especially when the target data source does not provide native preservation functionality, or data would not be properly safeguarded against modification or deletion in the target system (this is especially true for ephemeral or mobile data sources). Thus, the legal and compliance standards that apply to the duty to preserve ESI inherently flow through to the process of collecting that ESI.

Regular Review of Legal Holds

Legal holds must be monitored and reviewed regularly to confirm that all relevant custodians, data sources, and systems are included. The legal hold notice is essential for notifying individuals of their duty to preserve data. A proper legal hold plan includes reminders and release notices.

Existing data may change or new data may be created during the data collection phase.d. Consequently, periodic follow-up reminders should be used to help custodians understand their ongoing preservation responsibilities. A best practice would be to issue reminders monthly or quarterly, depending on the matter's complexity.

Once litigation is complete and legal holds are released, timely release notices prevent the unnecessary retention of data, allowing data to be defensibly deleted based on the organization's standard retention policies.

Chain of Custody

The chain of custody establishes and documents data's movement, access, and integrity from its collection to production and potentially as exhibits at trial. Maintaining an unbroken chain of custody during the data collection phase is critical for proving the data has not been altered or tampered with.

Proper documentation during preservation and collection is essential for maintaining chain of custody. This helps identify who collected the data, what data was collected, when it was collected, and from where it was collected. This documentation also includes each data transfer, providing information on timestamps and the individuals involved.

Hash values (digital fingerprints) are generated during collection to validate data authenticity. These unique values ensure no changes occur throughout the eDiscovery process. These hash values can be cross-referenced with the original source data to verify collection completeness.

Regulatory Considerations

Global organizations, or organizations that store data globally, require special handling of ESI, focusing on awareness of jurisdiction and regulatory requirements. Privacy laws stipulate strict controls for processing personal data and provide certain consumer protections. Others provide stringent safeguards around sensitive data, such as healthcare records.

These regulatory restrictions must be considered when collecting custodial data. Due to privacy laws, you may be required to redact or anonymize sensitive personal information. Any privacy compliance measures taken at the collection stage must also be clearly documented and reported to the compliance team.

Global data residency or sovereignty laws may restrict data transfer across borders. Identify data residing in jurisdictions with data residency requirements and collaborate with legal and IT teams to establish protocols for data transfer while complying with local laws. Implementing encryption and secure access controls for data storage and transfers helps to mitigate compliance risks.

Jurisdictional Requirements and Forensic Certification

In some jurisdictions, the prevailing practice may be hiring a certified forensic examiner to collect data, even if the organization has in-house eDiscovery collection tools. The examiner or consultant can use the organization's tools to provide a forensically sound process and documentation. Some states even have statutes requiring individuals to possess certain licenses, such as a private investigator's license, to collect third-party devices, so be sure to check local laws before hiring a consultant.

Another reason many companies rely on forensic examiners or third-party solution providers for non-standard data types -- such as mobile device data, social media data, or ephemeral data -- is that the examiner can later testify (and be certified) as an expert to defend the integrity of the data collection. Third-party providers also ensure the review of personal devices with with the custodian's privacy in mind, preventing fellow employees access to a custodian's personal data not relevant to the matter.

Common Challenges in Collection

A collection plan cannot be complete without anticipating and planning for potential issues. Despite robust planning, challenges in collection are inevitable, particularly given the complexity of modern data ecosystems. These roadblocks may hinder the eDiscovery workflow, adding time, cost, and risk to the collection process.

Implementing the tools and techniques from previous sections—IG, identification, and preservation—can overcome most logistical and technical challenges. All the processes throughout the initial stages of eDiscovery pave the way for a successful collection of ESI.

It is essential to plan for and have a strategy to address potential issues when they are encountered. This chapter introduces these issues and we provide more information about tools and techniques to address them in the next chapter.

Diverse Data Sources

New data types, such as data from emerging technologies like collaboration apps, ephemeral messaging apps like Snapchat and

Signal, or closed-ecosystem cloud storage applications, may present unique hurdles for data collection.

Older systems or archive data sets may store data in formats that are difficult to access or convert for downstream review. Accessing these data sources often involves navigating permissions, encryption protocols, and potential cross-jurisdictional legal issues.

Logistical and Technical Challenges

Managing data effectively within large organizations presents several significant challenges which must be addressed to ensure successful and efficient collection processes. The sheer volume of data produced and stored in large organizations is a primary concern. Without proper data management strategies, collection teams can quickly become overwhelmed, leading to delays, inefficiencies, and increased costs. Organizations generate data from many sources, such as emails, databases, cloud storage, and collaborative tools, all adding complexity to the collection process.

Data integrity is another critical issue during the collection phase, mainly when dealing with sensitive or volatile data sources. Ensuring the data remains unaltered is vital, as any modification could compromise its reliability, validity, and admissibility in legal proceedings.

Data access poses challenges, as relevant information can be dispersed across numerous systems, devices, and geographic locations. Access to these diverse data sources often requires coordination between IT, legal, compliance, and operational teams. Additionally, data may reside in legacy systems, or proprietary platforms that complicate extraction or under the governance of strict regulatory or contractual access controls, further delaying the collection process.

Human Factors

Human factors play a critical role in eDiscovery, particularly in how employees and departments interact with data and one another. One prominent factor is *custodian behavior*. Employees may inadvertently or intentionally obscure data sources by using unauthorized tools such as personal devices, external storage platforms, or unsanctioned cloud applications. This behavior can complicate legal and IT teams' data identification and collection processes. Employees may not realize the risk of bypassing approved systems, such as the potential for non-compliance with data retention policies or increased data spoliation risks during litigation.

Seamless communication between legal, IT, and business units is essential for efficient eDiscovery workflows, yet achieving this level of collaboration can prove challenging. Legal teams often lack the technical expertise to articulate their needs to IT teams, while IT professionals may not fully understand the legal context surrounding eDiscovery requests. This misalignment can result in delays, incomplete identification of electronically stored information (ESI), and increased legal risks.

Conclusion

In this chapter, we explored the critical stage of collection within the eDiscovery workflow, emphasizing its role as the bridge between preservation and downstream analysis. The importance of accuracy, defensibility, and efficiency when gathering electronically stored information (ESI) was underscored. We highlighted the significance of strategic planning, collaboration between legal and IT teams, and the careful scoping of collection efforts to avoid unnecessary costs and risks.

Key considerations such as custodian-based collection, content-specific culling, chain of custody, and proportionality were examined to ensure defensible and efficient data collection processes. Finally, we addressed emerging challenges like diverse data sources, ephemeral and mobile data, and compliance issues in cross-border data handling. Effective collection ensures the integrity and reliability of ESI and sets the stage for a streamlined and cost-effective eDiscovery workflow.

What's Next

In the next chapter, we explore the tools, techniques, and methods that make defensible and efficient collection possible. Building on the strategic foundations from this chapter, we will cover:

- Developing a Collection Plan: Best practices for ensuring a structured and defensible approach to gathering ESI.
- Collection Techniques and Methods: From targeted imaging to remote collection, we will explore various methods suitable for modern data ecosystems.
- Advanced Tools for Data Collection: Automation and validation techniques to enhance collection efficiency.
- Handling Emerging Data Sources: Strategies to tackle challenges posed by cloud-based platforms, mobile devices, and ephemeral messaging apps.
- Documentation and Transparency: Maintaining defensibility through comprehensive audit trails and proper chain of custody practices.

Chapter 8 will equip you with the technical expertise to address collection from complex data environments while adhering to legal and regulatory obligations.

Chapter 8 - Tools and Techniques for Data Collection

This chapter expands on the key principles outlined in the previous chapter and provides a framework for developing and implementing efficient, defensible, and accurate data collections in your eDiscovery workflow.

Key Themes

- Developing a Collection Plan
- Addressing Practical Challenges
- Selecting Collection Methods
- Utilizing Advanced Tools and Techniques
- Documentation and Risk Mitigation

Pre-Collection Planning

Proper planning is a critical first stage of the collection process, ensuring the retrieval of ESI is defensible and aligned with case objectives. As with any other project, proper planning ensures the collection is executed efficiently and accurately.

Assemble a cross-functional team consisting of members from legal counsel, IT staff, and data stewards. This team should collaborate to define the scope and parameters of the data to be collected and provide diverse expertise, allowing them to address technical, legal, and organizational challenges that may arise during the collection process.

This initial step involves reviewing any custodian mapping and data mapping tools or output to gain a thorough understanding of custodians and potential data sources. This allows the team to prioritize efforts and optimize resource allocation. Understanding these sources—whether they are cloud storage platforms, email servers, or physical devices—provides the foundation for effective scoping.

Scoping is critical to focusing efforts and avoiding unnecessary overreach. It starts with reviewing and validating custodian interviews. Validating this information highlights existing data sources, may uncover overlooked repositories, and provides essential context for the data's role in the matter.

Next, review and validate the data map, which leverages existing inventories to identify data locations and their technical configurations, such as structured databases or legacy systems. Risk assessment is integral to scoping to ensure the collection avoids improperly exposing sensitive information or technical hurdles that could jeopardize compliance or efficiency.[9]

Finally, draft a formal collection plan detailing all this information for reference during the collection and as a record of the decision process. The collection plan records the data sources and custodians, timelines and deadlines, required tools and techniques, documentation, feedback, and risk mitigation strategies should issues arise.

---

[9] As you review data sources for potentially sensitive or protected information, including proprietary or confidential information that could have a detrimental commercial impact on the organization if shared, the team should consult with counsel to determine whether a protective order should be drafted as well as the categories of information that would be included in that order.

Address Practical Challenges

After verifying the custodians and the data that needs to be collected, identify any challenges that could hinder the collection. These include challenges mentioned in the previous chapter, such as navigating encrypted, ephemeral, or unconventional data sources, which demand specialized tools and expertise. Encryption enhances data security but complicates accessibility for collection. Ephemeral data—designed to be temporary, like certain messaging apps—adds urgency to data preservation efforts. Additionally, non-traditional sources, such as IoT devices, social media, or collaborative tools, often lack structured frameworks for discovery and evidentiary integrity.

Agreements must be arranged with custodians to recover relevant content from these applications. Other challenges include access to data sources, indexing limitations, and export format. Assess each of these, as they will help determine if you can provide a complete collection internally or need assistance from an external expert.

Determine Collection Method

For any data that may be difficult to collect, consider hiring an external Legal Services Provider (LSP) or certified forensic examiner to assist you with the collection.

If an organization needs to collect data from a source infrequently or finds the required tools prohibitively expensive, it might choose to hire a third-party expert experienced with that data source and who can serve as an expert witness if needed.

In some cases, internal teams may have the resources to collect data from the data sources in scope, including data sources with efficient search and export functionality.

For each data source, determine whether ESI will be collected by an internal team, an external expert, or if the internal team will need to procure additional tools to complete the collection.

Internal Collections

If you determine you can perform the collection internally, you must take important steps to ensure its completeness and defensibility. From the moment data is identified as potentially relevant, every action taken must safeguard its authenticity, protect against spoliation, and support the legal team's ability to demonstrate compliance with preservation and collection standards.

The techniques and methods outlined below provide a roadmap for achieving these objectives.

Tool Selection

Working from the collection plan, identify tools that allow you to access the data as required for the matter. Identification and preservation provides information about the custodians and the scope of the data. During collection, you must use tools and processes to collect and prepare the data for review.

Earlier, we mentioned some data sources may be capable of exporting data for simple collection. These may include cloud file repositories and file-sharing platforms. Others, such as messaging and collaboration applications, may require specialized tools for collection.

Explore each data source and application for search and export capabilities. Does each provide the information you need to satisfy your collection process specifically related to metadata and content?

If you determine the native tools will not suffice, choose which tool best satisfies your collection needs. Add this information to your data map so you always have an up-to-date list of tools for each data source or application. Documenting, updating, and reusing this information for future matters streamlines the entire eDiscovery process, reducing costs and risk.

The following list is incomplete, as responsive data may reside in other sources. Going into depth on each data source or application on the list could be a book of its own, so we provide an overview here. To get more detailed information on data collection and forensics, we suggest the book *Forensic Data Collections* by Robert Fried, ISBN 979-8884173026, available atwww.forensicsbyfried.com.

Cloud Storage Services

Data from cloud storage platforms like Google Drive, OneDrive, or Dropbox can be collected using native APIs or specialized eDiscovery tools such as Cloudficient CaseFusion. These tools allow for extracting metadata, files, and, in some cases, file versions and deleted files. Look for tools capable of preserving folder structures and associated metadata.

Mobile Devices

Mobile device data, including texts, emails, photos, and app data, can be collected using mobile forensic tools such as Cellebrite, ModeOne, or Oxygen Forensics. These tools extract logical or physical data, ensuring relevant data, such as GPS locations or chat application data, is preserved. Ensuring compatibility with various mobile operating systems and addressing encryption or security features, such as PINs or biometric locks, is essential.

Legacy Archives

Legacy archives, such as decommissioned systems or obsolete storage formats, may require specialized tools or services to extract data. Techniques include migrating data to modern platforms or using emulators to access proprietary software. Companies like Cloudficient provide migration expertise and modern data platforms to support legacy archives in eDiscovery workflows.

Collaboration Applications

Platforms such as Microsoft Teams, Slack, or Confluence require tools that integrate via APIs to extract data, including messages, shared files, and audit logs. eDiscovery platforms like Cloudficient CaseFusion, Relativity, or Exterro offer targeted capabilities for collecting data from these sources while maintaining metadata integrity and contextual relevance.

Instant Messaging and Chat Applications

Messaging apps like WhatsApp, Signal, or Telegram pose challenges due to encryption, decentralized storage, and very short server-side retention (meaning the only viable copy of the content may reside on the physical devices used to send and receive the messages). Tools like X1 Social Discovery or Hanzo can collect chats and associated attachments. Collaboration with custodians is often necessary to obtain decryption keys or export content directly from the app on device.

Laptops / Desktops

Forensic imaging tools like EnCase or FTK (Forensic Toolkit) can create exact copies of hard drives from laptops or desktops. These tools preserve system logs, file access histories, and deleted files, which can be crucial depending on the circumstances of the matter. Investigators using these tools will document each step and use write blockers to prevent alterations to the source device. Forensic images act as a protective container preserving all aspects of the target device for later review, as if it were frozen in time. Not every matter requires full forensic imaging of end-user devices, and it may not be required for every custodian. While creating your collection plan, discuss with counsel whether exact duplication of the entire device is required or if remotely retrieving individual files from the device is sufficient. Cases involving intellectual property, criminal activity, data breaches, and fraud may require this level of forensic collection.

Email Servers

Email servers like Microsoft Exchange or Google Workspace support native exports and integrate with third-party eDiscovery tools to extract emails, attachments, and metadata. Perhaps the most mature of eDiscovery tool integrations, several tools can integrate with email servers to perform target searches and native file export using APIs.

Network Drives

Data from network drives can be collected using indexing tools or direct forensic collection methods. Tools can assist in identifying relevant data through keyword searches or metadata filters. Ensure file paths, permissions, and timestamps are preserved.

Social Media Platforms

Data from platforms like LinkedIn, Facebook, or X (formerly Twitter) often requires using APIs or specialized tools like X1 Social Discovery. These tools can capture posts, messages, and associated metadata. Obtaining consent and complying with platform terms of service are important considerations, especially for content that contains images or mentions of unrelated persons.

Physical Media

Forensic imaging tools like FTK Imager or dd (a Linux-based tool) clone physical media like USB drives or external hard drives. Data is extracted while ensuring write protection to maintain the original state. Proper labeling and chain-of-custody documentation are essential for defensibility.

Data Backups

Data stored in backup systems can be restored using native backup tools, such as Rubrik, Cohesity, or Commvault, or eDiscovery tools to extract specific files. Organizations like S2Data provide services for storing and retrieving legacy backup data that may have outlived the native backup tools. Care must be taken to address deduplication and ensure the restored data reflects the original state. Audit trails and validation reports help ensure defensibility.

Business Applications

Data from business applications, such as CRMs or ERPs, is often accessed using database queries or application-specific export features. Tools like SQL Server Management Studio or proprietary extraction utilities provide structured data in formats suitable for legal review. Documenting the query logic and data extraction processes is essential.

Proprietary Systems

Proprietary systems often require collaboration with the system vendor or IT team to access data. Export methods can include custom scripts or API integrations. Care must be taken to document data structures and ensure available metadata and system logs are preserved for defensibility.

Inaccessible Systems (When All Else Fails)

Sometimes exporting data will simply not be possible or could be very expensive and/or time consuming, making the effort unduly burdensome. In rare cases, parties will agree to let the requesting party access the system in very controlled environment. In the days of paper discovery, these setups would be called "reading rooms." The producing party's IT team and/or counsel monitor the process to ensure no unauthorized data is accessed beyond what was agreed. We mention this to emphasize that there are often multiple solutions to a collection challenge, and the method used may end up being a compromise agreed to by all parties and approved by the court. That compromise may look very different from the typical forensic workflow.

Tool Selection Best Practices

You probably noticed a few names appeared multiple times in the section above. Once you have analyzed the data sources and applications needed to interrogate for relevant data and added those tools to your data map, look for areas where single tools can provide collection across multiple platforms or data sources rather than point solutions for each one.

Tools like Cloudficient CaseFusion and Expireon provide data identification, preservation, and collection solutions. They allow users to collect against many data sources, such as legacy archives (via automated migration protocols), file servers, cloud-based storage, and collaboration applications.

Other tools, such as forensics collection for mobile devices, can also be used for laptops, desktops, physical media, and backup devices. Forensic imaging creates bit-by-bit copies of data and captures active files, deleted files, and hidden content. Forensic tools also keep valuable metadata intact, allowing the capture of creation dates, ownership information, and modification history.

Collection Scenarios and Techniques

After selecting the tools for the collection, determine how to collect the data. This includes scenarios such as custodian-based or content-based collection and whether the collection can be performed remotely or requires being onsite or physically present near the data source.

Custodian-Based Collection

Data collection requests, usually adapted from the original requests for production sent by opposing counsel, are generally constructed to favor broad retrieval rather than precision, often resembling the following: *Give us all data for these five custodians between these date ranges in these three data sources*. Custodian and data mapping tools are utilized, along with custodian interviews. Once this data is collected, it is passed downstream for review tools to cull further cull the data using analytics and keyword searches.

Optionally, if the data is collected into a centralized platform, such as Cloudficient Expireon or a similar tool, keyword searches can be completed as part of an Early Data Assessment (EDA) exercise. Even though keywords are used to cull data sent to downstream review, the collection's focus is still custodian-based as it was initiated with a custodial focus.

Content-Based Collection

There may be some instances where custodians cannot be determined, so the collection focuses on certain keywords or terms across certain data sources. This data collection request may resemble something like: *Collect all data related to Project Phoenix across these five data sources.* In this instance, you would center the collection on content related to Project Phoenix, using keyword filters and metadata searches to quickly narrow the scope of ESI to be collected.

Remote and On-Site Collection

Modern workplaces often require diverse approaches to data collection. Remote collection tools, often provided by API-driven third-party solutions, enable teams to access data from geographically dispersed systems without disrupting operations. On-site collection is invaluable for capturing data from specialized systems or mobile phones.

Ensuring Data Collection Authenticity and Defensibility

Arguably, the most important aspect of data collection is maintaining data integrity throughout the process to guarantee the accuracy, downstream usability, and authenticity of evidence. Forensically sound collection methods are critical. Hashing algorithms such as MD5 or SHA-1 generate unique digital fingerprints that can be checked at each stage of the eDiscovery workflow to ensure the data remains unaltered through production.

Comprehensive logging tools and digital signatures document the chain of custody and record every interaction with the data, thus preserving the integrity of evidence and enabling legal teams to validate data with opposing parties and the court.

Defensibility hinges on consistent and well-documented processes. During the collection, legal teams must implement repeatable data collection and validation procedures. Regular audits of the chain of custody confirm compliance with legal and procedural requirements, alleviating risks of missing or improperly handled processes. Reviewing and documenting errors or exceptions generated during the process further enhances the credibility of the collection.

Focusing on authenticity and defensibility forms the foundation for handling collected data, ensuring compliance with legal standards while minimizing risks of spoliation or admissibility challenges.

External Collections

Using an external firm, such as a legal services provider, for eDiscovery data collection can be strategically beneficial in scenarios where in-house capabilities or resources are insufficient or when expert testimony may be required. Below is an overview, key factors, and advice for selecting an external provider.

When to Choose an External Firm

Complexity and Scope of Data

Large or diverse data sources like cloud, mobile, and legacy systems may require specialized tools and expertise. Sophisticated or hybrid environments may exceed in-house capabilities.

Defensibility and Compliance

External firms ensure strict adherence to legal and technical standards, reducing risks of spoliation or mishandling, and often maintaining the robust documentation and audit trails crucial for defending against scrutiny.

Cost-Benefit Analysis

While external services may seem costly, utilizing their services reduces downstream review costs by enabling targeted collections and/or refining collected data ahead of processing and review. A firm's expertise in leveraging automated tools for culling and filtering data contributes to cost efficiency.

Resource Constraints

Organizations with limited IT or legal staff may lack the bandwidth or expertise to execute large-scale or time-sensitive collections.

Technical Challenges

Data that spans multiple jurisdictions with varying privacy and legal requirements or involves emerging formats, such as IoT and ephemeral data, often requires external expertise.

What to Look for in an External Firm

Proven Expertise

Verify experience with similar industries or cases, especially regarding data types and legal contexts.

Advanced Technology

The firm should utilize up-to-date tools for legal hold management, automated collection, and complex data handling.

Certifications and Compliance

Check for organization-level certifications, like ISO 27001, for data security or compliance with GDPR, HIPAA, and other relevant standards.

Transparency and Reporting

The firm should offer clear processes, regular updates, and detailed reporting to support defensibility.

Scalability and Flexibility

Ensure the firm can scale services to your case's demands and adapt to evolving data or legal requirements.

Collaborative Approach

Look for a partner willing to collaborate with your legal and IT teams to align efforts and optimize workflow.

Staff Credentials

The firm's consultants or forensic examiners should have the credentials needed to be certified as an expert if required to testify. Examiners should also hold any certifications or licenses required to perform forensic collections in the applicable jurisdiction.

Contracts

Before any work is performed, review contracts and agreements carefully to ensure satisfactory liability limits, indemnification, confidentiality, and data handling (including the use of AI and cybersecurity standards).

Documentation and Transparency

Whether you choose an internal or external collection, documentation and transparency are critical components of any defensible data collection process, especially in the legal context of eDiscovery. These principles ensure compliance with legal obligations and help defend against claims of misconduct, negligence, or spoliation of evidence.

Organizations that use internal data collection must create a reliable audit trail of their actions by systematically recording each step of the data collection process. Organizations that choose external data collection must ensure the external collection vendor provides the same. Internal and external collection efforts rely on common objectives to ensure defensibility.

A cornerstone of defensibility is establishing a clear and thorough audit trail. This audit trail must document all actions taken during data collection, including who accessed the data, when it was accessed, and the methods used to secure and preserve it. The meticulous nature of this process is designed to uphold the integrity of the collected information, ensuring it remains untampered and can withstand scrutiny in legal proceedings.

Several types of documentation are typically required to satisfy these standards. Chain of custody forms, for instance, track the movement and handling of data from its origin to its final storage. These forms provide a sequential record confirming the data's authenticity and reliability. Additionally, data collection logs detail every technical and procedural aspect of the process, offering insights into the tools and methodologies employed.

Standardization and Continuous Improvement

Once the collection process is complete, these lessons can be incorporated into a broader IG framework, ensuring the organization is prepared to meet future legal and compliance demands. Effective IG frameworks integrate transparency and documentation as foundational principles, streamlining the eDiscovery process and mitigating potential legal risks. This is a great way to provide a feedback loop to the IG team, making future eDiscovery efforts more efficient.

Standardized templates for collection activities significantly enhance consistency and efficiency. Whether capturing custodian interviews, logging chain of custody, or validating collected data, templates help ensure no critical steps are overlooked. Regularly updating these templates to reflect new legal precedents or emerging technologies aligns your processes with industry standards.

By adhering to these methods and leveraging the right tools, organizations can confidently approach data collection, knowing their efforts meet legal requirements while minimizing risk. Effective data collection is not just about gathering information—it's about doing so with precision, transparency, and defensibility.

Getting Started and Quick Wins

Because the collection is reactive, the initial thought may be that you cannot do much to get started proactively, but there is a lot you can do to prepare. The first three parts of this book provide essential guidance to make the collection as efficient as possible, but a few key tasks can help you prepare for the actual collection.

Create a Cross-Functional Team

Creating the collection team does not wait to for a collection request. Plan ahead and identify a collection team, including members from legal, IT, compliance, and business teams, to address diverse challenges.

Determine members using the guidance from the previous chapter. Then, conduct a kickoff meeting to align goals and define roles, emphasizing collaboration.

Just as IT forms cross-functional teams to prepare for disasters or security incidents, the collection team can be ready to act when called upon for a pending matter.

Conduct Pre-Collection Planning

Review custodian and data maps to identify potential data sources and prioritize them based on relevance. Validate custodian interviews and data mapping exercises to uncover overlooked repositories and avoid unnecessary overreach. Add information to the data map based on custodian and data source information discovered from the planning sessions.

Begin testing data sources and applications to determine the level of effort to search and export data from each one. Document findings and determine which applications can meet the collection needs natively, which applications or data sources require a third-party solution, and which ones may require help from an LSP or forensics group.

Run Mock Collection

Begin testing data collection processes and perform practice runs of mock cases before you are presented with a real matter. This exercise allows you to address any issues that may arise while you are not under pressure to produce data on a strict timeline.

For data sources that provide native functionality that meets your collection needs, test the process and document your findings. Then, export the data and verify its authenticity and defensibility, as described in the previous chapter.

For data sources that may require a third-party solution or help from an LSP, contact software vendors, and LSPs to begin researching the tools and expertise needed to collect from those data sources. Use guidance from the previous chapter to help you determine whether you buy tools to perform internal collections or use an LSP to assist you with an external collection. Many organizations follow an 80/20 rule to determine how much data they can collect via internal collection and native and third-party tools versus how much they will need to use an LSP.

Sometimes, an organization can handle data collection internally by investing in a few key tools, reducing the need for external assistance. By acquiring and implementing these tools proactively—before a legal matter arises—they can ensure readiness and efficiency when the need occurs.

Create Documentation Templates

Create templates to document the collection process, such as:

- The overall collection plan
- Chain of custody forms or logs
- Consent forms for accessing personal devices
- Exception handling logs

Many of these documents will need to be reviewed by in-house and possibly external counsel, so it is best to create them before collection begins as an active matter.

Unify Data Collection with Technology

Deploy automated tools for remote data collection for high-profile targets. For example, if you know email will always be collected in every matter, start archiving email to a central location to save collection time.

Adding multiple data sources to the archive can benefit this process. If other high-profile targets are added to the archive, you will benefit from a faster, centralized collection process, unifying the search and export tasks. Instead of learning to identify custodians and data, set preservation, search, and export from multiple tools, each with its processes, you can perform all those tasks from one platform and provide a unified experience for all data.

Solutions like Cloudficient CaseFusion and Expireon provide the best of both worlds: a proactive archiving platform plus a platform for point-in-time collections from multiple data sources.

Initiate Data Access Logs

Enable audit logs on high-profile data early to anticipate any matters that may target them, then monitor those logs for data access to maintain defensibility. Proactive access log monitoring starts tracking information, allowing future efforts to benefit from more historical data. Regularly review access logs to identify compliance risks and gaps and provide that information to the company in a feedback loop.

Launch Communication and Reporting Dashboards

Reporting dashboards allow you to share progress and successes with stakeholders, building confidence. Use simple visual formats to highlight metrics such as storage cost reductions or compliance milestones. While the term "dashboard" may sound complex, its creation can be accomplished simply with a shared presentation file or a project management application like Asana.

Conclusion

This chapter reviewed the importance of strategic planning, practical problem-solving, and leveraging appropriate tools in the data collection phase of eDiscovery. A well-developed collection plan forms the foundation for defensible practices, ensuring the process remains accurate, efficient, and aligned with legal and compliance standards. By addressing potential challenges and implementing best practices, organizations can enhance the reliability and defensibility of their eDiscovery workflows, ultimately supporting successful case outcomes.

What's Next

As we transition from the electronic discovery (ESI) collection phase, Chapter 9 will introduce the tasks required to prepare data for downstream tasks, such as processing, review, and production. These steps mark a critical shift from data collection to preparing that data for use in litigation.

Key topics in the next chapter include strategies for processing ESI, considerations for privilege and protective orders, and the construction of effective review workflows. You'll also gain insight into techniques for leveraging technology-assisted review (TAR) and advanced analytics to manage costs and improve efficiency. This chapter sets the stage for understanding how properly processed and reviewed data supports case strategy and ensures compliance with legal requirements, leading ultimately to successful productions. Together, these elements will guide you through the operational and legal considerations that shape the preparation for review and production, ensuring you're ready for the challenges ahead.

.

Part V: Downstream Review Processes

Chapter 9: Preparing for Review

Key Themes in This Chapter

- Processing ESI
- Search terms
- Privilege considerations
- Protective orders
- Review workflows
- Productions

Now that we have covered information governance through collection of ESI, we come to the next set of steps, referred to by many as the "right side of the EDRM." This divide between collection and the remaining phases (processing, review, production, and presentation) mirrors the divide between tasks handled internally by corporations, using corporate-owned tools, and those outsourced to third-party vendors or law firms.

The primary reason for this is likely that document review platforms were, historically, owned or licensed by law firms or service providers. During that time, managing servers for tools like Summation, Concordance, or Relativity was expensive, requiring specialized expertise, and a variety of processing and imaging tools to convert data into compatible formats.

Today, with modern SaaS platforms like DISCO, Everlaw, and RelativityOne, it is becoming more common for enterprises to license the platforms themselves. Professional services, offered by the vendor or a third-party service provider, bridge the gap for data processing and production.

In this chapter, we will address each of the "right side" phases except presentation, which simply refers to the post-production process of preparing exhibits for trial or other proceedings. This process is very case-specific and involves marking exhibits, then strategically choosing how to present items (electronically, physically, via video, etc.).

Since this book's focus is on foundational eDiscovery, we are combining these final phases into a single chapter, but they form the basis for what could become an expanded second edition in the future. If you would like for us to release an expanded second edition, let us know! Our contact information is in the front of this book.

Processing ESI

After its collection, the ESI must be processed before review. Processing involves several steps usually performed in sequence by a specialized tool or set of tools. At a high level, processing involves:

- Extracting container files like .zip or .cab, then retrieving embedded files (such as a spreadsheet embedded into a presentation). This is an important step to ensure all files are indexed and searchable.
- Indexing electronic documents to ensure all content and metadata is loaded into a database like Elastic. This index is used for searches, analytics, filters, and machine learning algorithms during review.
- Converting data into formats that support a better review experience. For example, chat data from Slack is typically exported in JSON format which, without conversion, is not usable by reviewers. Relativity has

created a specific format for chat data called Relativity Short Message Format (RSMF).

- Constructing message threads and document families. This includes all types of messages – emails, chats, and mobile device messages. During review, you can save time and gain valuable context by examining a full conversation. RSMF or other short message renderings can be viewed as they appeared in the native application, giving reviewers full context to evaluate the conversation.
- Performing OCR on any non-searchable images such as TIFF or PDF files. Doing so makes those files searchable in the review platform and allows the extracted text to be produced with the image file following review.
- Handling exceptions, such as unsupported files or those that failed to process. These exceptions should be documented, and if the original file is corrupted, it should be retrieved and reprocessed, if possible. In some cases, files may be encrypted or password-protected. If so, the end-user or company's IT team may need to provide credentials to decrypt the file before processing. It is important to address these exceptions as they occur to maximize the likelihood that corrective action can be taken.

Pre-Processing

Each review platform has its preferred file formats for ingestion, so processing often includes a step called "pre-processing." This involves filtering out system files or unsupported formats, narrowing the data collection by date range or custodian, and converting data into a supported format if necessary (e.g., converting chat data to RSMF).

Pre-processing can also help reduce costs if the organization did not or could not perform a targeted collection. Once the data is scanned by the pre-processing tool, some of it may be marked to skip during the processing step. This means less data is uploaded to the review platform, reducing the volume of files attorneys will need to review. With review accounting for almost 80% of total litigation costs, any reduction in total data to be reviewed can lead to significant cost savings.

Some tasks performed in pre-processing include:

- **Organizing and staging data:** Collected ESI can flow to a service provider over time, and if it comes from multiple source systems, it may not be organized in the most efficient manner for processing (by custodian in folders, etc.). Also, if the data is transmitted in a compressed format (like .zip files) to protect metadata and improve transfer speeds, it must be extracted before processing. This can take quite some time depending on the overall size of the data corpus.
- **DeNISTing and file type filtering:** DeNISTing involves comparing the hash values of all files to a list of known system files published quarterly by the National Institute of Standards and Technology (NIST), then removing them from the processing queue. Additionally, ther file types may be filtered out by extension or by types that are irrelevant but not yet captured on the NIST list.
- **Date range filtering:** Often, the review date range may not be fully known at the time of preservation or collection, or the organization may choose to do a

custodian-based collection without a date filter. Reducing the overall date range can dramatically reduce the volume and hosting costs of the review.

- **Custodian filtering:** Not all collected custodians need to be processed immediately. In some cases, both parties may agree to a phased discovery approach to reduce costs. This involves first producing documents from key custodians and then revisiting in a second phase once the first data set has been reviewed by the receiving party. Also, more custodians than ultimately required may have been preserved and collected because the scope narrowed following the Rule 26(f) conference.

Preparing for Processing

Preparation for processing can start as early as information governance (proactively) or preservation. As you are working with IT to build your data map, both at an organization level and case level, it is important to understand how data will be preserved or exported for collection. Review that information with your processing vendor as early as possible to understand impacts on time and cost. One seemingly simple decision or option when exporting data could have a big impact.

Search Terms

One of the tasks performed by the system processing ESI is building an index. Despite advances in analytics, machine learning, and AI, keyword search terms are used in most eDiscovery cases today (2025) to isolate potentially responsive documents for review. To maximize recall (retrieving ***all*** the responsive documents), practitioners tend to sacrifice precision (getting ***only*** the responsive documents). Wildcards and other methods are used in the search syntax to make sure the net is cast wide. Analytics like filters, topic clusters, near duplicates, message threading, and machine learning can help refine those results.

Where searches are performed is vitally important. As we have mentioned in prior chapters, search features and indexing are different across source systems like Microsoft Exchange Online or Slack. And they will be different yet again for any forensic tools used to collect data from mobile devices or laptops. Search terms used to cull the data corpus for review should always be run AFTER processing, in the review platform, to ensure consistent results. If you are using keyword search terms to perform targeted collections ahead of processing, ensure that you fully understand the limitations of the source system's index and search capabilities to make sure you are not in breach of an ESI protocol or other agreement related to searches.

A search's output is called a search term report (STR), which provides a count of documents/items containing hits for each term. This report can be very valuable when iterating on search terms and sampling results. In an employment case with a large shipping company, one of the authors was asked to use the term "age" and realized this resulted in thousands of documents being included that were "vessel age reports." This is a great example of a term needing to be refined (ex. "age AND <plaintiff name>").

Search processes should be agreed upon in the ESI protocol. Do not agree to search terms until you have processed the collected data and sampled results from terms. Search terms almost always need iteration to achieve the most precision possible with complete recall. Collaboration is key when refining search terms. Use STRs and insight from sampling results to argue that terms are too broad or should be refined. Everything is easier with evidence.

Privilege Considerations

The attorney-client privilege is a well-known protection but not typically well-understood by non-lawyers. In eDiscovery, it is a tricky and complex issue requiring careful consideration both in planning and execution to protect against inadvertent disclosure of privileged materials to opposing parties. Imagine an email or chat thread outlining your case strategy or sensitive advice from counsel pops up in the opposing party's review platform! Whether that party can use such information depends upon several factors we will explore further.

Rule 502

The Federal Rules of Evidence (FRE) work in conjunction with the Federal Rules of Civil Procedure (FRCP) to provide procedural guidance used and interpreted by courts to settle disputes, including in discovery. FRE 502[10] applies to disclosure of a communication or information covered by the attorney-client privilege or work-product protection. This rule covers disclosure, waiver of privilege, inadvertent disclosure, and several exceptional circumstances. One of the most important provisions is 502(d): "Controlling Effect of a Court Order." This provision allows parties to enter into an agreement, later memorialized in a court order, to protect the parties from

---

[10] Fed. R. Evid. 502

inadvertent disclosure and allow the parties to *claw back* disclosed privileged materials if discovered.[11] Getting the agreement incorporated into a court order to provide maximum protection is very important.

We recommend taking the time to have a 502(d) Order entered in every case, even if the discovery effort seems light. As new data types and cross-app conversation threads become the norm, early detection of privilege will become more difficult. Human reviewers are not perfect, so it is always possible for something to get accidentally included in a production.

Absent a 502(d) Order, section 502(b) outlines the requirements to avoid waiver of privilege once disclosure has been discovered. There is quite a bit of caselaw on this topic, and as always, look for recent cases in your jurisdiction that give some insight into what the court would consider "reasonable steps" taken to prevent disclosure.[12]

Privilege Logs

When documents are determined to be privileged or protected work products, they will be tagged in the review platform for later retrieval and special handling during production.

However, you cannot simply exclude those documents if they otherwise meet the criteria for relevance and would otherwise be responsive to the opposing party's discovery request. FRCP

---

[11] *See* Fed. R. Evid. 502(d). *See also* Fed. R. Evid. 502(e) ("An agreement on the effect of disclosure in a federal proceeding is binding only on the parties to the agreement, unless it is incorporated into a court order.")

[12] *See* Fed. R. Evid. 502(b)(1)-(3) (Test for determining whether privilege has been waived upon disclosure of privileged materials.)

26(b)(5) discusses handling of privileged or protected materials in discovery and requires that in order to withhold information on the basis of privilege, the party must "expressly make the claim" and "describe the nature of the documents, communications, or tangible things not produced or disclosed – and do so in a manner that, without revealing information itself privileged or protected, will enable other parties to assess the claim."[13]

Following this rule in practice leads us to the privilege log, a document that tackles the difficult task of providing enough information for a party to assess the claim of privilege without disclosing the privileged information. This often means providing metadata for messages or associated document family member information for documents. If an attorney is the sender or a recipient, there is a good chance the message is privileged. That is, of course, not always the case, but at massive scale, parties are generally not able to thoroughly evaluate privilege claims for every document when they appear, on their face, in the privilege log to be privileged. Metadata alone is not sufficient, however. According to the rule, you must "expressly make the claim" for each item withheld.[14] This means that you must add a comment to the privilege log describing why the item is protected. This is usually a short summary of the contents.

Typically, attorneys will configure their document review platform to capture all the information required for the privilege log while reviewing items for privilege. We will discuss review

[13] Fed. R. Civ. P. 26(b)(5)(A)(i)-(ii).
[14] Fed. R. Civ. P. 26(b)(5)(A)(i).

workflows in more detail below, but when preparing documents for privilege review and identifying potentially privileged materials, the typical workflow involves running several searches using a set of terms. These include words commonly found in privilege disclaimers, attorney names and email addresses, and other relevant keywords. Advancements in AI provide a promising future where this process is much more streamlined, reducing the margin for error. For example, Cloudficient Expireon can categorize items as potentially privileged upon ingestion into the archive. These items can then be tagged during export or exported in a separate batch during collection to expedite the privilege review process. Generative AI is also being tested in review platforms to create privilege log comments, but at the time of writing, feedback from practitioners concludes that generative AI still has a long way to go before it can completely take the place of attorneys writing privilege log comments.

Partially Privileged Documents and Redaction

What should you do if only part of a document or communication is privileged or contains sensitive information? We recommend redacting the privileged or protected content (including metadata if applicable) and producing the partially redacted item. This item is then referenced in the privilege log.

Today, it is not necessary to spend a lot of time finding adequate redaction technology, as it has become commoditized as a service that can be quite easily embedded into software. However, this was not always the case. There are horror stories from years past where redactions were reverse engineered, or where you could simply highlight the redacted area of a file and copy the text hidden under the black boxes. The authors are both old enough to remember a time when a Sharpie marker was the primary redaction tool.

The most important thing to remember about redaction is that native files generally should not be produced if an item needs to be redacted. In that case, even if native files are agreed upon as the form of production for one or more filetypes, you still need to produce image files for the redacted items (or a placeholder image for a document or page that is fully redacted). You should then omit the native version of that document in the production. There are few review platforms able to redact information from native files like spreadsheets because these files are generally requested in native format. Make sure you understand how the redaction of native files works in that platform and that you are confident the redacted information is truly gone. You should also review the file in native form outside of the review platform to once again confirm all information that should be redacted is truly removed. Every popular review platform has general redaction capabilities and should be able to produce a redacted image of documents.

What do you do if an email communication is privileged, but attachments to that email are not privileged and are otherwise responsive? If those attached documents are not produced individually or as attachments to another communication, then they must be produced. To accomplish this, you would likely need to redact the entire communication or insert a placeholder but produce the attachment unredacted with the family relationship still intact. In the privilege log, you can mention whether the attachment has or has not been redacted in a comment or in a dedicated column/field. To determine whether the attachment would otherwise be produced or is contained elsewhere in the review corpus, you could leverage analytics in your review platform like near duplicate analysis or run a very specific keyword search on a large portion of the document content to find a match. This should be a condition that you look for in your privilege review – even creating a tag perhaps for "attachment not privileged" so you can retrieve these outliers easily at any time.

Protective Orders

Like privilege protection, a party may also request protection from disclosing materials that could cause some sort of injury or burden on the disclosing party (or the subject of the information).[15] Frequently, this protection is used for materials that are proprietary or confidential. It can also be used to allow redaction of PII or PHI to protect the privacy of employees, customers, or other individuals whose data is contained in the documents. Parties generally attempt to agree to a plan for handling these materials, including any of the following scenarios impacting eDiscovery:

- **Special designation or routing of materials:** Documents are marked with an "Attorneys' Eyes Only" (AEO) designation to ensure the plaintiff does not get to view the materials. This is common in cases involving business competitors, where confidential or trade secret information is contained in the discovery materials.
- **In camera review:** Documents are sequestered and provided directly to the court for review by the judge. This prevents opposing counsel from seeing the details

---

[15] *See* Fed. R. Civ. P. 26(c).

of the documents until the court can evaluate the protection claim. This option can also be used in disputes over privileged items where the opposing party cannot evaluate the claim of privilege based on the information provided in the privilege log.

- **Redaction:** If only part of an item requires protection, it can be redacted just like partially privileged documents.
- **Withholding items from discovery:** Completely withholding an item requires a log, like the privilege log, that asserts the claim for each document. The process for asserting these claims should be specified in the order.

There are many other scenarios where protective orders are used in litigation. In this chapter, we only wanted to provide a general understanding of how this may impact eDiscovery and how to plan for the review process. Any time trade secrets or sensitive data are being transmitted, parties should seek a protective order based on the circumstances of the case.

Review Workflows

This brings us to document review, currently the most expensive phase of discovery, representing about 80% of litigation costs. In this phase, attorneys review documents collected and processed in a review platform, tagging and categorizing them as they review. Costs can include platform hosting for the data, analytics or AI being used, and an hourly or per-document rate for the reviewers.

For the producing party, document review serves many functions:

- Learning the case facts and formulating strategy

- Determining what is responsive and must be produced
- Classifying documents by issue or for deposition prep
- Looking for privileged or protected items and entering justification
- Redacting privileged or protected information

For the requesting party, review serves one primary purpose: to help build their case against the producing party and allow their claims to survive dispositive pre-trial motions. They also will review for deposition prep, computing damages, and other purposes.

Let's explore costs for a moment. It is difficult to fathom the enormity of the costs involved in eDiscovery until you break down review costs. Cloud-hosted review platforms are usually priced based on capacity used and billed per month until the case is archived or taken offline. These rates run from $5 to $40 per GB. They may also include user fees for reviewers as well as a charge for expanded data capacity (for example, a PST file containing email data could expand 2-3 times when all items are processed). For a 10 TB case, billed at $5 per GB on the expanded data set, the hosting cost alone would be over $1M, assuming a 2.5x expansion rate. Fortunately, you can cull data during pre-processing or with search terms pre-review to reduce the long-term cost of hosting.

In addition to hosting, expenses include the rate for attorney reviewers. The lowest rate for contract reviewers we have seen is around $50/hour, but this rate can be as high as $400+/hour, depending on which level of attorney performs the review. The typical reviewer can review around 60 documents per hour in first pass review. Therefore, if you have 1 million documents in a review workspace (after initial culling), reviewers will need to spend more than 16,000 hours reviewing those documents at a *minimum* cost of over $800,000. This does not include fees for more experienced attorneys doing privilege review or quality control. That could push the review expense closer to $1 million. Large enterprises send and receive millions of messages per day, so you can imagine how large (and expensive) these data sets are to review and how much those costs will rise over the next several years.

Let's explore some common review scenarios.

Who is Reviewing?

Who reviews the documents can vary by case or phase. Client preferences or efforts to reduce costs in large matters can impact these decisions, and each phase of review may require different levels of experience or familiarity with the subject matter of the case documents.

In-House Reviewers

For smaller matters, such as EEOC charges or internal investigations, in-house attorneys or paralegals may perform document review themselves. They also may be required to review documents later in the matter to help assess confidentiality or provide subject matter expertise for technical or specialized documents. Non-lawyer subject matter experts from business units may also be required to review documents containing proprietary information to help the legal team understand impacts on case strategy.

Law Firm Reviewers

The most common type of reviewer is an attorney at the law firm representing the producing party. Although these attorneys are likely the most expensive, they also tend to have the most detailed knowledge of the case and a strong understanding of the client's business. They also may have previously represented the organization in similar matters. Even if contract reviewers are used for first pass review, law firm attorneys will likely be used for advanced stages like privilege review and to perform quality control on the first pass.

Contract Reviewers

Reviewers contracted for a particular case are referred to as contract reviewers. They are licensed attorneys who work for a vendor that specializes in seating review teams for eDiscovery document review on a project basis. One of the benefits of contract reviewers is that the team can, if needed, scale up quickly to accelerate review pace. It is harder for law firms to hire one or several full-time employees to scale up for a single case. However, several law firms do operate dedicated review centers, and those firms are able to scale up quickly and handle very large cases.

Contract reviewers are usually utilized for the initial review of documents for responsiveness and issue coding (categorizing the documents based on relevance to the issue(s) in the litigation). Contract review teams are managed by a higher-level attorney, who usually also works for the vendor, and the entire process is managed by a case attorney. Contract review rates are almost always less expensive than attorneys at a law firm – except perhaps if the firm has its own review center operated like a vendor.

The case team develops a review protocol and holds a kickoff meeting with the contract review team to discuss review objectives and provide details about the key issues in the case.

They use analytics and reports and direct quality control to supervise the whole process. Since vendors regularly handle large-scale review projects, they may offer review management expertise and tools that surpass the capabilities of law firms providing an opportunity for small-to-medium sized firms to scale for a project that would have otherwise been impossible.

The only downside to using contract reviewers is they generally only work on a particular client's case once, so they are not as familiar with the content or the case as in-house counsel or the case team. However, if managed properly, with adequate supervision and access to case team attorneys for assistance when needed, contract review teams can be a very cost-effective way to manage a large document review.

How are They Reviewing?

Linear Review

As the name implies, linear review is a workflow where attorneys simply review one document after the other until there are none left to review. This is usually combined with some use of search terms or other analytics like message threading to speed the process up a bit. It is probably the least efficient method of review, but it is the most comprehensive.

Technology-Assisted Review

An argument can be made that Technology-Assisted Review (TAR) is more accurate than human linear review. This is technically true, but it is highly dependent on the tools being used and the team managing the review. TAR involves the use of machine learning algorithms to detect similarity in documents so that, after appropriate training, the trained model can predict other documents likely to be responsive. This is very effective for prioritizing the review. You can calibrate the settings to a point you are comfortable the system has found all responsive documents. Generally, you should also sample a subset of documents not identified as responsive to increase confidence that all responsive documents were found.

Many review platforms offer some flavor of TAR. Older versions were called "predictive coding." Since precision is important in eDiscovery and the prevalence of responsive documents in a data set is usually low, a very large number of items needed to be reviewed to train these legacy systems before any predictions could be made. Today, continuous active learning models are more common. These models feed reviewers better and better documents as they review so they do not have to sequester a random set of documents for dedicated training and then wait as the model is updated. This is all done on the fly, and platforms like DISCO dynamically update review batches with responsive documents, improving review outcomes and reducing cost.

Combining active learning with analytics that group documents, such as threading, can increase confidence that all responsive documents have been discovered without needing to do a linear review of 100% of the documents.

AI

The use of true AI in review is in its infancy, but platforms are already releasing AI-enabled tools in their review platforms. The ability to query evidence and retrieve documents based on natural language queries is very helpful when preparing for depositions and hearings, writing briefs or motions, and performing other tasks requiring rapid access to case facts and context. For a receiving party, the ability to query productions early can be a huge strategic advantage.

Structure of Review

First Pass

First pass review, as the name implies, is the initial review of all documents matching search terms or other criteria included in the review corpus. During the first pass, reviewers make decisions related to general responsiveness to discovery requests and categorize documents based on relevance to issues in the case. This is commonly referred to as *issue coding*. Reviewers tag documents with appropriate labels for issues and/or responsiveness. Other tags available during first pass review could include "needs further review," "technical issue," "hot document," and even "potentially privileged." Throughout the review, the review managers and case team attorneys look at documents with these secondary tags to address processing/formatting issues and quickly surface hot/important documents to the case team.

Quality Control

Quality control, or QC, is extremely important when managing any size review team, but is especially important when managing a larger team, such as a blended team of contract reviewers and case team attorneys. QC involves a series of steps that may vary depending on the sophistication of the review platform and team.

First, in almost every review, there will be some level of re-review – that is, examining a sample of the documents reviewed by the first pass reviewers to test for accuracy and understanding of the review objectives. In some platforms, because active learning models are already predicting for relevance, those scores can also be used to predict documents that should be examined for QC. Many platforms also include simple sampling functionality that allows review batches to be created from a random sampling of the documents already reviewed. If managing a larger team, attorneys performing QC should ensure they get a sample of each reviewer's work.

Quality control should be performed throughout the project, not just at the end of first pass review, and the number of overturns or tag corrections per reviewer should be tracked. If that number is high across the team, it may be an indication the team needs to be retrained immediately, and the review protocol should be updated for clarity. If a single reviewer has a high number of overturns relative to their peers, then the team manager should engage with that reviewer to determine what is causing the higher number of overturns.

To ensure the team understands the review protocol and is making accurate decisions, a higher number of resources may be dedicated to QC during the first or first several weeks of first pass review. It is much easier (and cheaper) to retrain the team after a few days of review than to recode millions of documents later. As confidence increases, QC batches and resources may be reduced to begin working on other phases of review.

Privilege and Advanced Review

Documents protected under the attorney-client privilege, work product protection, or by a protective order must be separated and marked before production to ensure they are not inadvertently disclosed. Many of these documents will need to be redacted as well if they are only partially protected. In modern review platforms, redaction is built into the platform and, for most of the documents, will be completed by a senior member of the case team.

How the documents are separated or flagged may vary by platform, but the result should be the same: the documents marked as entirely privileged or protected will not be produced with the other documents in the case, and the documents that are partially privileged or protected will be produced with those sections redacted and the associated extracted text omitted.

It is common practice to use search terms to isolate potentially privileged documents. These terms are typically built from names of all legal team members, internal and external, who worked with the organization during the relevant period of the case along with other terms such as "privileged," "attorney client," or "work product" among many others that may refer to specific legal processes used by the organization or its law firms.

AI-based categorization or privilege detection is becoming more commonplace as technology evolves. It is even possible to detect privileged documents in IG using a platform like Cloudficient Expireon, which can predict privileged content at the point of preservation and collection to bolster the overall defensibility of the steps taken to prevent inadvertent disclosure.

Pre-Production Quality Control

Before documents are produced following review, the case team or their litigation support team performs one final spot check of the documents marked for production. This includes sampling to ensure production specifications are adhered to, ensuring there are no errors in the production preview, reviewing redactions for accuracy, looking at larger spreadsheets or other complex files to be sure they are rendering as expected (or flagged for native production), and looking for any contradictory tags or folder inclusion (for example, an unredacted document tagged potentially privileged but also in the production folder).

Productions

After review is complete or as phases are completed, the producing party will create a production. This is the term for the collection of items that will be submitted to the requesting party. In some cases, there may be just one production, but in larger, more complex cases, the parties may agree to rolling productions, meaning batches of documents will be produced on a rolling basis until all documents have been produced.

Many review platforms have production features built in, but professional services teams or litigation support professionals usually manage the process and handle exceptions like large format files requiring special rendering outside of the primary platform.

The most important elements of productions are the form and manner of production. Parties should agree on form and manner of production at the outset of the case, preferably when negotiating the ESI protocol, or if there is no ESI protocol, when drafting the scheduling order. Knowing how you need to produce ESI helps your entire team plan more effectively and ensures that you receive discovery from opponents in a manner you expect.

Form of Production

Form of production refers to the form or format of the documents or files shared in discovery. With ESI, this could mean native files, image files (usually .tiff or .pdf), or a combination of both. However, there are many other elements that should be discussed and included in an ESI protocol or other agreement:

- **Load file:** A load file is just a collection of metadata and references to the files included in the production. It helps link native files, image files, and extracted text. Most review platforms accept .DAT load files (sometimes referred to as the "Concordance" load file format after the original eDiscovery platform that used it). You should request a format compatible with your review platform.
- **Metadata:** What metadata will be included in the load file? Make sure to request everything needed to properly display the production in your review platform as well as take advantage of any analytics.
- **Redactions:** How will redacted or withheld files be handled? Will there be placeholder images in the production for withheld documents?
- **Extracted text:** You will need extracted text for the files to be searchable in your review platform. The receiving

party could OCR them, but it is generally easier to just include the extracted text with the production.

- **Document families:** How will document family associations be referenced? By document ID? Ensure that family associations are maintained in the production and discuss how hyperlinked files will be handled.

Many law firms have their own production specifications, and federal agencies like the Department of Justice and the Securities and Exchange Commission have production specs that must be followed when responding to discovery requests. Work with your law firm or review vendor to be sure that you are addressing form of production early in the case. Do not wait until it is time to start producing documents.

Manner of Production

Manner of production refers to how you will deliver the production. Will you transmit it electronically using SFTP or a cloud-to-cloud data transfer utility? Or on physical media? Productions have deadlines, and you need to account for the manner of production in your overall eDiscovery timeline. If transmitting electronically, the source or destination internet bandwidth may not be adequate to send massive productions of multiple terabytes. In that scenario, you may elect to send the production on encrypted physical media.

Data security is another important consideration for manner of production and eDiscovery generally. Ensure the data is encrypted, passwords or keys are provided separately, and that the data will be stored at the destination securely. In several surveys of law firms performed by the American Bar Association (ABA), law firm cybersecurity practices and technology were found to be lagging those of their corporate clients. For particularly sensitive data, you may want to negotiate a more specific security protocol. It is probably at least worth asking how the data will be stored and if any third parties will be accessing the data.

Receiving Productions

When you receive a production, you should quickly validate the production is complete and is intact – that is, the files are not corrupt and can be loaded into your review platform.

Also, the production could include several hyperlinked files in emails or chat messages. If you want to request these documents or they were supposed to be included per the ESI protocol, time is of the essence since those files are likely stored in users' active cloud file shares. Some may have been shared from third parties, and a subpoena would be required to get these files. Being able to analyze a load file/production within hours of receiving it can help ensure you have the best chance to get important documents and gain valuable insight into the contents of the production.

Production analysis tools like Cloudficient Hyperlize can identify all the hyperlinked files/modern attachments for produced messages and determine whether they are included in the production or not. It can also sort them by cloud tenant, so you can quickly tell if those files were shared by the producing party's employees or by third parties. Hyperlize also validates other aspects of the production, allowing users to make changes to the load file or create overlay files for items received after the original production. This early insight ensures documents from opposing parties can be obtained before they are deleted and that third-party subpoenas if needed, can be issued in a timely manner.

Conclusion

We included this chapter as an introduction to processing through production. Even though this book's focus is foundational eDiscovery, it felt incomplete without discussing these topics. There is quite a bit more to learn on these topics, and we hope to expand on them in a future edition or future volume. If you are an eDiscovery professional who works more with the foundational eDiscovery phases (IG through collection), you can use the information in this chapter to help you prepare for the downstream phases and think about ways to optimize costs or streamline processes.

Can your collection processes or tools be updated to prepare ESI for processing and reduce the amount of conversion needed or perform DeNISTing and pre-processing of content in house? Can the successful implementation of IG practices and defensible deletion of data reduce the total volume of data that will be preserved, collected, processed, and ultimately reviewed? Based on the review costs discussed in this chapter, any steps you can implement from this book's previous chapters to defensibly reduce the volume of data to be reviewed will lead to significant cost savings.

Use the concepts in this chapter to ask questions of your vendors, outside counsel, and peers to better understand the implications of each decision you are making in eDiscovery projects. As you can see, decisions early in the case can have a big impact on outcomes and costs later. And remember that each case teaches us something that we can use to improve a process, ask better questions, or improve the quality in the next case.

Chapter 10 - Conclusion: Bringing It All Together

As we have explored throughout this book, effectively managing the foundational stages of eDiscovery - information governance, identification, preservation, and collection - is essential for organizations to mitigate risks, control costs, and ensure defensibility in the face of litigation and regulatory inquiries.

Key Takeaways

1. **Foundational Role of Information Governance (IG)**
   Information governance serves as the bedrock, enabling organizations to proactively manage their data in a manner that aligns with business, legal, and IT priorities. By establishing robust IG frameworks, organizations can streamline eDiscovery processes, reduce data volumes, and enhance compliance with legal and regulatory requirements.

2. **Criticality of Identification**
   The identification phase builds upon this foundation, connecting custodians, data sources, and case facts to pinpoint relevant ESI. Techniques such as custodian interviews, data mapping and leveraging advanced eDiscovery tools can significantly enhance the precision and efficiency of identification efforts.

3. **Preservation for Defensibility**
   Preservation is critical for maintaining the integrity and

defensibility of ESI. Implementing legal holds, documenting processes, and employing defensible collection strategies help organizations meet their duty to preserve while avoiding the pitfalls of spoliation.

4. **Strategic Collection Practices**
   The collection phase, while often reactive in nature, benefits greatly from strategic planning and the use of cutting-edge tools and methodologies. By assembling cross-functional teams, tailoring collection plans to case specifics, and leveraging both internal resources and external expertise as needed, organizations can ensure that their collection efforts are targeted, efficient, and legally defensible.

5. **Quick Wins and Long-Term Strategies**
   Each chapter has highlighted quick wins—immediate, actionable steps to improve workflows—as well as long-term strategies to build sustainable practices. Together, these create a roadmap for organizations to elevate their eDiscovery maturity.

The Path Forward

The evolving nature of data and technology ensures that the eDiscovery landscape will continue to shift. To remain effective, professionals must embrace adaptability, invest in training, and leverage emerging tools and methodologies. Collaboration across legal, IT, and business teams is no longer optional but essential.

By integrating the principles and practices outlined in this guide, organizations can not only navigate the complexities of eDiscovery but also turn it into a strategic advantage. Whether facing litigation, regulatory inquiries, or proactive risk management, this framework offers a foundation for success.

As you apply these insights to your unique challenges, remember that continuous improvement is key. Reflect on what works, refine your processes, and remain committed to excellence. The journey through eDiscovery is ongoing, but with the right tools, mindset, and collaboration, it can be navigated with confidence.

Glossary of Legal and eDiscovery Terms

Active Learning: A type of machine learning used in Technology-Assisted Review where the system continuously learns from reviewer decisions to improve document categorization.

Attorney-Client Privilege: A legal protection that keeps confidential communications between attorneys and their clients.

Chain of Custody: Documentation that tracks the movement, access, and handling of electronically stored information (ESI) from collection through production to maintain data integrity.

Collection: The process of gathering electronically stored information (ESI) identified and preserved for eDiscovery purposes.

Contemporaneous Version: The version of a document as it existed at a specific point in time, particularly important when dealing with hyperlinked files in collaborative platforms.

Custodian: An individual who creates, receives, or manages electronically stored information (ESI) relevant to a legal matter.

Custodian Mapping: Documenting and understanding the relationships between custodians and their data sources, including historical information about roles and responsibilities.

Data Mapping: Identifying and documenting where data resides within an organization, what retention policies apply, and how data flows through the organization.

DeNISTing: The process of removing system files from an ESI collection by comparing file hash values against the National Institute of Standards and Technology (NIST) list of known system files.

Early Case Assessment (ECA): The initial evaluation of a case's merits based on identified data and custodians.

Early Data Assessment (EDA): The process of analyzing collected data to understand its content and scope before full processing and review.

Electronically Stored Information (ESI): Any information created, stored, or transmitted in digital form.

ESI Protocol: A detailed agreement between parties in litigation that outlines how electronically stored information will be handled throughout the discovery process.

Form of Production: The format in which documents or ESI will be produced in discovery (e.g., native files, image files, or a combination).

Hash Value: A unique digital fingerprint generated for a file that can be used to verify its integrity and authenticity.

Hyperlinked Files: Files referenced via hyperlinks in emails or collaboration platforms rather than traditional attachments.

Information Governance (IG): The framework of policies, processes, and controls that govern how an organization manages its data throughout its lifecycle.

Legal Hold: A written notice requiring the preservation of potentially relevant electronically stored information when litigation is reasonably anticipated.

Load File: A file that contains metadata and references to documents included in a production, used to import documents into review platforms.

Manner of Production: How produced documents will be delivered to the requesting party (e.g., electronic transfer, physical media).

Metadata: Information about electronic documents such as creation date, author, modification history, and other properties.

Native Format: The original file format in which a document was created and maintained.

OCR (Optical Character Recognition): Technology that converts images of text into machine-readable text.

Preservation: Ensuring that potentially relevant ESI is protected from alteration or deletion.

Privilege Log: A document listing items withheld from production due to privilege claims, including sufficient details to assess the claim's validity without revealing privileged information.

Processing: The phase of eDiscovery in which collected ESI is prepared for review by extracting text and metadata, creating searchable indexes, and converting files to reviewable formats.

Production: Providing processed and reviewed ESI to opposing parties in litigation.

Protective Order: A court order that protects confidential or sensitive information from disclosure or limits its use in litigation.

Redaction: Removing or obscuring sensitive or privileged information from documents before production.

Rule 26(f) Conference: A mandatory meeting between parties to discuss discovery plans, including ESI handling, as Federal Rules of Civil Procedure requires.

Rule 502(d) Order: A court order that protects against waiver of privilege through inadvertent disclosure of privileged materials.

Search Term Report (STR): A report showing the number of documents containing hits for each search term used in document review.

Spoliation: The destruction, alteration, or failure to preserve evidence when under a duty to do so.

Technology-Assisted Review (TAR): The use of machine learning and analytics to assist in document review and classification.

Work Product: Materials prepared by or for attorneys in anticipation of litigation, protected from discovery by the work product doctrine.

Index

Made in the USA
Columbia, SC
07 March 2025

0eaaee2a-b51e-4a05-b532-2f79d939f037R01